Touching

A History of Deafblindness in Scotland

by
Drena O'Malley

Contents

Foreword

It is an honour to be asked to contribute a foreword to this history of deafblindness in Scotland painstakingly researched and written by Drena. This is essentially a story about the inspirational people who contributed to the history by making a difference to the lives of deafblind people not only in Scotland but in the UK and indeed all over the world. Drena is no exception and she can take pride in the progress made in her native Scotland since she answered Deafblind UK's call in 1989 and started as Liaison Officer working part-time to set up the Scottish office. Her role was to support deafblind people across Scotland and the first deafblind person she met was Dorrie Moore. Dorrie was an inspirational deafblind lady who retained a great sense of humour and zest for life into her eighties, despite having to cope with deafblindness for more than half her life. I have been lucky enough to meet and work with both ladies and I well remember when I first met Drena in 1998 while working for Shell Exploration and Production in Aberdeen. Her passion for supporting and enabling deafblind people in Scotland was energising then and remains so. She inspired me to become a member and make my own small contribution to the story. I've never regretted it and have met so many inspirational people, whether deafblind, guide/communicators, volunteers or staff members, some of whom are mentioned in these pages. I hope you enjoy this history as much as I have and my thanks go to Drena for all her work in pulling the story together, for all those who helped her and of course to her rock, Hammy, who has supported her and many deafblind people over the years, including me.

Bob Nolan, Chair of Deafblind Scotland, 2001–19

Acknowledgements

The creation of this book would not have been possible without the help of many people over the years, too many to list here, however, I must thank all of the deafblind people who contributed to the history; your contribution is irreplaceable, as was your encouragement to keep going over the years. Staff, former staff, guide/communicators, and volunteers from Deafblind Scotland have answered questions and clarified information over the period, and for that I am truly grateful.

Supporting me throughout the process has been former employee of Deafblind Scotland, Allan Clark, who has become a good friend of mine. Allan worked for Deafblind Scotland for several years and we worked to create chronologies which listed what happened when, and who was involved. These were used to give accurate information and shape to the history. This kept us right as we tried to make the account as factual as possible, based as it is on documents of all kinds, from that time.

However, a particular debt of gratitude is owed to my long-suffering husband Hammy whom I told in 2017 that I should be able to finish the book in 3 months, 6 at the most. That was just as the new building was reaching completion and just before he was diagnosed with Lymphoma, which I'm delighted to say he recovered from. However, this diverted both of us for many months. Then in 2018 I had an emergency operation on my back, and couldn't sit for any extended period for many months. That too diverted both of us. The rest, as they say, is history. Hammy supported my work with deafblind people and the organisation for almost 30 years. It is no surprise that he has supported my efforts to finish this book.

There have been a number of stumbling blocks along the way while writing this book and I am grateful for the support of deafblind people who pushed, encouraged and supported me to get it to the end.

Deafblind Scotland has always been supportive of my efforts and will continue to offer support by creating excerpts from the book in Braille and Moon, thereby making it accessible to deafblind people. I am very grateful to the board of directors and staff for enabling this to happen.

Strathkelvin Talking Newspaper Association volunteers have kindly offered to help create an audio version of the book. And it is hoped to create a BSL version using both Deaf volunteers and BSL interpreters. If we are successful with all these plans this book might become one of the most accessible books for deafblind people in Scottish history, which would be a source of great pride to everyone involved.

Introduction

This book came about following a project, funded by the Heritage Lottery Fund, to develop a history of deafblindness in Scotland. The aim was to produce a historical account which was accessible to deafblind people and to involve deafblind people in its creation. The large history boards in the hallway of the Learning and Development Centre are a result of this project and are regularly used by deafblind people and others. Deafblind people also told their own stories, some of which are included in this book. A chronology of important events was developed for the library, together with a short history for each of the past 30 years.

I felt there was a need to take it further and have written in this book about the part deafblind people played in shaping recent deafblind history, and the effect of legislation and other events over the years. It is hoped this book will be of interest to deafblind people themselves, to professionals working with them and to those who wish to better understand deafblindness.

I have included chapters on deafblindness and on communication to ensure information on the unique nature of this disability is available to all. I have also written about the "Field of Dreams" project to build Deafblind Scotland's new Learning and Development Centre, as little information is available about such a project. And "Field of Dreams" was a historical undertaking for Deafblind Scotland and its members.

Acquired deafblindness is not a subject which has a rich literary heritage so I have used information from a wide range of sources to tell the story, as well as drawing on my personal experience over a 30-year period. I hope this book will lead to greater understanding about the lives of deafblind people, their culture, and their history.

The hyphen in "deaf-blind" was removed in 1991, in a Europe-wide decision. This was done to show that this was a separate, distinct disability, and not just blindness added to deafness. For simplicity I have used the term "deafblind" wherever possible. In a similar vein the name National Deaf-Blind Helpers' League (NDBHL) was changed to National Deaf-Blind League (NDBL) in 1989–91 and for the same reasons we will refer to it as NDBL throughout.

The history of deafblindness, however, is mainly about people, about deafblind people themselves and how they overcame the challenges they faced. And about those who helped them. We will, therefore, begin with the stories of individuals.

Chapter 1

Deafblind heroes from history

Throughout history there have been partnerships between a deafblind person and a sighted-hearing person, which enabled deafblind people to grow, develop, thrive, to make an impact in their local community, or on the wider world. This history looks particularly at the people and the situation in Scotland. However, the world of deafblindness is a small one, and therefore it is important to include deafblind people from other countries who helped shape the deafblind world. You may know some, and never have heard of others, but I hope you will find their stories inspirational.

There is little doubt that Helen Keller is the deafblind person with whom most people are familiar, and her story is known across the world. America is the place where deafblind education was first developed. Helen's story, told below, together with that of her tutor, Anne Sullivan, inspired many across the world to take an interest in the communication methods which might be used with those who have a severe dual sensory loss. However, Helen had a number of forebears worthy of mention.

Scottish history is peppered with mentions of deaf sign language users. In terms of deafness, the first person in Scotland recorded as using sign language was **Joan Stewart**, Countess of Morton, who was born in 1428, the daughter of James I, King of Scotland, and known as the mute lady of Dalkeith. Although there are written accounts of deaf children and how they communicated and were educated – or not as the case may be – it is not until the early 19th century that mention is made of a deafblind person in Scotland.

David Gilbert Tate

1: A cottage typical of David Gilbert Tate's

David Gilbert Tate was reported by Dr Sam Hibbert in the *Edinburgh Philosophical Journal* in 1819 as "A lad born deaf and blind in the Shetland Isles". Reportedly, in 1794, Hibbert was undertaking a study of rocks at the time when he was told of this young man on the island of Fetlar. He is described as having an "idiotic" appearance, having no sight and unable to walk upright. The youngest of 10 children he was described as living in a hovel in one of the poorest parts of Shetland. His parents did not believe it was worthwhile to give him any kind of teaching. He moved along slowly on all fours and was badly stooped when Hibbert met him. He had little or no useful communication and spent his time by the fire moulding soft clay into different shapes.

James Mitchell

2: James Mitchell

James Mitchell was born deafblind in 1795 in Nairnshire, one of 7 children, and useful information is recorded about him. He quickly developed touch, taste, and smell in a way which allowed him to distinguish any of his belongings from those of a stranger. He was known to rattle objects against his teeth, producing a vibration which travelled to the brain, the nearest approach to sound he was ever to enjoy. It was said that, "the faculty of intellect he certainly possessed in a considerable degree". He used signs and gestures to communicate with a supportive family by imitating movements, activities, or characteristics. A pat on the head signified the "highest approbation". His family indicated a wait of 3 days by closing his eyelids and putting his head in a sleeping position 3 times. His father was a minister, which may well have aided his socialisation. In his rural community there were always friends willing to act as a guide to him and he developed a taste for walking, running, and riding horses. He sought outdoor pursuits whenever he could. After his father's death the family moved to Nairn and, with the help of 19th-century guides, Jamie slowly and carefully researched routes, walking distances of 10–15 miles on a regular basis. He was given hospitality wherever he arrived from congenial hosts, many of whom understood his basic signs. And many of whom knew his liking for hot food on arrival. He died aged 73 in 1869.

Julia Brace

Julia Brace (1807–84) was the first deafblind child documented as being in any kind of schooling in the USA. She was recorded as using familial tactile sign language as a child after she became deafblind at age 4 due to typhus. As a young adult she attended the American School for the Deaf and quickly became proficient in tactile use of standard signs. However, she was older, therefore it was thought that the cost of a formal education for Julia could not be justified. However, Dr Samuel Gridley Howe visited Julia in 1841 when she was 34 years old, bringing with him Laura Bridgman who was 12 years old and using one-handed manual alphabet. Julia was willing to learn and was enrolled at Perkins Institute for the Blind. However, after a year it was agreed she preferred to use sign language rather than the one-handed alphabet and it was agreed she should go back to Hartford Asylum for the Deaf and Dumb to live as part of their community. She entered into community activities and became part of its life, knitting, sewing, and carrying out tasks on a daily basis. In 1860 she moved to Bloomfield to live with a married sister.

Laura Bridgman

Laura Bridgman (1829–89) was another child from the USA who became a trailblazer for deafblind people. Laura's family was stricken by scarlet fever in 1831 when Laura was barely 2 years old. Two of her sisters died and Laura was left deafblind, and with no sense of taste or smell. She used a primitive set of signs to communicate mainly with her mother. Laura became known to Dr Samuel Howe, director of the Perkins Institute for the Blind. He wanted to try to give Laura an education and in 1837 she went to the Perkins School. She learned English using raised letters and one-handed manual alphabet. Howe's interest lay in the fact that he wanted to shed some light on "the role that the senses play in the determining of human nature and creating human knowledge". At the age of 14, Anne Sullivan became her specialist tutor. It is interesting to note that the woman who was to become Helen Keller's famous tutor was first involved with Laura Bridgman. It is worth remembering that it was through reading an account of Laura Bridgman in Charles Dickens' *American Notes* that the parents of Helen Keller applied to the Perkins Institution for a teacher for their deafblind daughter. Having looked at the better-known individuals in history who were deafblind, it is indeed evident that the world of deafblindness is a small one.

Charles Howard Usher

3: Charles Howard Usher

Charles Howard Usher was not deafblind but was indeed a hero in that he discovered Usher Syndrome. He was born sighted-hearing in Edinburgh in 1865, and grew up to develop an abiding interest in inherited eye disease. He studied medicine at Cambridge and was first employed at St Thomas's Centre. He became a Fellow of the Royal College of Surgeons in Edinburgh and was employed as an apprentice surgeon in Aberdeen (1895–1926). His interest in inherited eye disease grew to include other genetic conditions. In 1913 he published a paper on Albinism, a genetic condition, and a year later he published a report to the Royal London Hospital on the inheritance of Retinitis Pigmentosa, describing associated deafness in some cases. He travelled the world and spent 2 years in military service in Salonika.

In 1935 he delivered the Bowman lecture on "A few hereditary eye conditions" evidencing his lifelong interest in the subject. And this is the reason why today we have a well-known condition in the deafblind community known as Usher Syndrome. C.H. Usher was the first doctor to research and identify it as a separate, genetic condition, which involved hearing loss from birth followed by sight loss in the teenage years.

Although much research has taken place, at the time of writing there is not yet a treatment which reduces the effects. C.H. Usher died in Edinburgh in 1942. There is an Usher collection in Aberdeen which illustrates the extent of his vital work in this field.

Helen Keller

Helen Keller was born in 1880 in Alabama and enjoyed normal development until she was 19 months old when she became ill with a fever, thought perhaps to be Scarlet Fever or Meningitis, which resulted in her becoming both blind and deaf. Alexander Graham Bell, well known as an activist in deaf education,

4: Helen Keller

recommended Anne Sullivan from the Perkins School for the Blind as the most appropriate person to try to establish communication with this very young girl. Helen Keller's mother read about Laura in Charles Dickens' *American Notes*. Dickens' written account of meeting Laura on his US trip ensured Laura was known worldwide. Thus, Anne Sullivan's place in the lives of these 2 deafblind people, and in history, was secured, re-enforcing that the world of deafblindness is small; in this case it worked well for both Laura Bridgman and Helen Keller.

Anne began work with Helen in March 1887, working with Helen to establish a connection between fingerspelling and objects; fingerspelling and activities; and between fingerspelling and English words. At this stage Helen's behaviour demonstrated great frustration with all around her, and in the end Anne and Helen moved out to stay in a small cottage on the family's estate in order to work on general behaviour as well as communication. This brought results and, a short time later, when at the family water pump, Anne persisted in putting Helen's hand under the running water, and then fingerspelling the word "water" onto Helen's hand. Anne was rewarded when Helen associated water running on to her hand with the fingerspelled word. Within hours Helen had learned the fingerspelling of 30 words and the objects associated with them. Three and a half months later Helen wrote a letter to her cousin Anna, "Helen write to Anna George will give helen apple simpson will shoot birds". Within months she was writing letters in fluent English to her mother.

Helen made many trips to the Perkins School, learning Braille and then some French, Latin, and German phrases. At this point she was also learning to speak, having felt the position of the tongue and lips on other people when they were speaking.

She went on to attend Radcliffe College, the women's branch of Harvard, and graduated with a bachelor's degree in English and German.

Helen enjoyed a 50-year writing career, travelling widely to promote her many books, which included *The Story of My Life* (1903) which was translated into 50 languages, *Helen Keller in Scotland* (1933), and *Helen Keller's Journal* (1938). In her travels she was accompanied until 1922 by her trusty companion Anne Sullivan, who retired that year. Helen then ventured into film, with *Helen Keller and her Story* winning an Oscar in 1957 and the play *The Miracle Worker*, which won the Pulitzer Prize in 1960. In the early 20th century, Laura Bridgman and Helen Keller established the principle that a fully deafblind child was able to be educated, and this principle was to prove a critical factor in the education of deafblind people for many years to come.

A very important part of Helen Keller's influence on Scotland's Deafblind Community was that the well-travelled Helen came on more than one visit to Glasgow. Evelyn Brown, who has Usher Syndrome, in her early years attended St Vincent's School for the Deaf and Blind, although long after Helen visited. In 2010, Evelyn wrote about Helen Keller and other famous blind people in a book in large print titled *Inspirational People* which contains the following:

"Between 1932 and 1955 Helen made a number of visits to Scotland. In 1932 she visited the following places:
June 15th – Glasgow University and Queen Margaret College
June 22nd – New Church of Scotland
June 23rd – Renfrew Street School for the Deaf
– Langside School for the Deaf
– St Vincent's School for the Deaf and Blind
One speech she gave to the deaf and blind children at St Vincent's School contained these words:

'You and I know that we are not deaf if we hear with our hearts. Our minds have their own eyes and ears, and if we think and feel right, we can plant flowers of contentment and happiness among the nooks and crannies of our limitations.

We are deaf only if we fail to find beauty and goodness in the world. But if we love the sun and the stars, the birds and the flowers, try every day to do something kind for someone, there will be joy for us on the mountains and fields; and in our lives there will be a sweetness that will overflow into the lives of others. These are the things that make everything in life beautiful.
Far away in the days to come is our goal. We may not reach it, but we can look up and see its beauty, believe in it and follow where it leads.'"

Helen died on 1 June 1968 and was buried alongside Anne Sullivan in the National Cathedral in Washington DC.

Chapter 2

Twentieth-century deafblind heroes and some sighted-hearing friends

Arthur Sculthorpe

5: *Arthur Sculthorpe*

Arthur Sculthorpe (1904–74) became deafblind in 1938 aged 34 and faced many years potentially cut off from communication. He was, however, determined to live as normal a life as possible. He became a skilled Deafblind Manual user, but was aware that most people do not know Deafblind Manual and he set out to change that, teaching thousands during his lifetime. However, using block capital letters printed on his palm as a direct means of communication he was able to quickly establish communication with the man in the street and over the years became a familiar figure in his home town of Peterborough. He had 3 guide dogs in his lifetime, all named "Sparkie".

Arthur was introduced to the founder members of NDBL, in Birmingham, which had been founded in

1928 by a small group of deafblind people and their friends. Arthur devoted all his energies to working with deafblind people, seeking to constructively help them to help themselves. He became editor of their magazine, *The Rainbow*.

He then captured the imagination of people from all walks of life when he made a radio broadcast in June 1948 appealing for funds for The League. Soon he was seen as the natural choice of deafblind people to become the next General Secretary of The League when the headquarters moved to Peterborough in 1950. He helped deafblind people to create better lives for themselves and worked tirelessly to influence statutory bodies and local authorities so that they might better understand the problems people faced when they became deafblind. He was awarded the MBE in the coronation honours in June 1953.

Arthur represented the United Kingdom as a member of the World Council for the Welfare of the Deaf-Blind Committee, at their first historic meeting held in New York in June 1957. During this visit he appreciated the message of encouragement printed on his hand by President Eisenhower: “Carry on the good work – Ike.”

Arthur wrote thus about the NDBL:

> “We are entirely independent as a result of having had the will and financial power to break through traditional ideas which stemmed from the false assumption that if you take an agency founded for the purpose of providing services for blind people with hearing, and combine it with an agency for deaf people with sight, you produce a body competent to deal with people who have the dual handicap of both deafness and blindness.” (from Joan MacTavish, BRAVO! Miss Brown: A world without sight and sound 1935–1973)

It was his dream to pioneer the building of self-contained flats for deafblind people so that, with a little support, they could live independent lives. Funds rolled in from the moment he broadcast an appeal in 1961. Thus, Rainbow Court, a housing complex built in Peterborough for deafblind people, became a reality in 1963. He received numerous awards for his achievements, working together with deafblind committee members. He had a private audience with Pope Paul VI in 1967, communicating with the Pope when he used block alphabet on Arthur's hand.

When he was commended for the success of the project at Rainbow Court, he lamented "it is no success story, for the battle is at its peak. I shall reckon I am a success only if and when the government produces the specialised service I am fighting for." He continued to fight for this specialised service until his death in 1974.

When I first started researching the history of deafblindness in Scotland, Arthur was described as being in close contact with fellow deafblind people, always ready to listen, advise, and encourage them to work towards a fuller life for themselves.

Later I learned about Mae Brown, a Canadian deafblind lady and about the part Arthur Sculthorpe played in her life and ambitions. He advised Mae that she had the ability to make a decisive difference to the prospects for deafblind people in Canada. He saw her difficulty as being due to being reliant on the Canadian National Institute for the Blind (CNIB), which for all its virtues was aimed at a single sensory impairment. He wanted CNIB to break from tradition and give her the freedom and backing to start a new service. He thought if that happened, she could accomplish anything. Like Mae, Arthur believed that deafblindness was a unique condition that required the attention of agencies employing people trained to understand and address the specialisms involved in a combination of sensory losses.

Arthur and Mae were regularly in touch, especially as she strived to get specialist services for deafblind people established in Canada. It is fascinating to me that deafblind people, devoid of the internet, mobile phones, and relying on Braille, could find each other, throughout the world, and be in contact with each other offering advice, support, and friendship. Arthur and Mae were just one example of that.

After Mae died, Joan MacTavish, Mae's tutor/intervenor, wrote a book about her life titled *BRAVO! Miss Brown*. The final chapter of this book is devoted to Mae, her struggles, and her achievements.

Dorothy Entwhistle

Dottie was born in 1938 and, until she was 13, could see and hear. Then she contracted Meningitis and, although she survived the illness, the effects were devastating; she was left both deaf and blind.

6: Dorothy Entwhistle

With remarkable spirit and determination Dottie embraced life again, determined to succeed in her education, in her career, and to make a real and lasting contribution to other people's lives.

Throughout her teaching career, she showed many young deafblind children, through her skill and her example, that the absence of both sight and hearing is a challenge that can be overcome. Rich, enjoyable, fulfilling, and interesting lives can be lived through the sense of touch.

Dottie joined Deafblind UK as an employee in 1989, and with typical energy devoted herself to making life better for thousands of deafblind adults. She toured the country tirelessly, visiting people in their homes, in residential care, in hospital. Wherever she went she lifted spirits and organised practical help that could really make a difference on the road to a better life for deafblind people.

We, in Scotland, knew Dorothy as Dottie. She started work just months before I did, and she was hugely encouraging to me, taking me under her wing at team meetings in Peterborough, when I knew little about deafblindness. She also visited Scotland many times, particularly in the early days when we were trying to make an impact, assisting with training in Glasgow in 1990.

She had previously worked as a teacher of deafblind children at the Pathways Unit in Condover School near Shrewsbury which used Makaton with its pupils. Several Scottish deafblind adults had attended Condover as youngsters and they were delighted to meet Dottie and to communicate with her in a relaxed way using Makaton These people lived far from Peterborough, in Aberdeen and Angus to name but 2, and she visited them more than once while also meeting them at deafblind events. Dorrie Moore, whose story is told below, just loved to see her, and they would communicate in Deafblind Manual oblivious to others around them.

She also made a point of making time to attend and speak at conferences in Scotland, including the annual Forum, a conference on deafblind issues where most of the speakers were themselves deafblind (see Chapter 9 for more about the Forum). And she had a soft spot for the Doers' Group which comprised younger adults in Scotland who liked to participate in more exciting activities like skiing, hillwalking, and going on holidays. Spending time on holiday with others who share your language and communication method is a real treat for deafblind people who often lead isolated lives. Dottie helped ensure a range of holidays were offered by the NDBL each year and that Scottish deafblind people be included in them. As membership numbers in Scotland grew the Scottish Office arranged 1 or 2 holidays each year which were very popular. We raised funds for guide/communicators to accompany deafblind people which meant members got some help with the costs involved. We skied in France more than once, cruised to Holland, visited Disneyland France, York, Scarborough, the Coronation Street set, and Cadbury's chocolate factory; we went youth hostelling, and walked the West Highland Way – well at least Avril Robertson from Fife did. Other deafblind members came along each day to support Avril's efforts. Holidays provided a real highlight each year. Then regulations changed which made holiday organising much more difficult. If we organised holidays for a group and paid as a group NDBL was viewed as a travel agent with all that involved.

Dottie still came to see us, and still travelled the world to speak at conferences and seminars, endeavouring to spread the word about deafblindness, and she trained thousands of people to understand more about deafblindness and to communicate with deafblind people.

With all this dedication Dottie was no pious saint – far from it! She had a wicked infectious sense of humour, loved a risqué joke, and followed rugby and football with an enthusiasm rivalled by few. Above all those who knew Dottie remember her as a warm, vibrant human being, and the world was a better place for having her in it.

Tragically, Dottie contracted a virulent cancer in 1997. Such was her desire to live that she battled with it ferociously and against all the odds. She persevered with every treatment and disfiguring surgery right until the end, and savoured every last drop of life.

She died in February 1999, aged 61, just 3 months after her official retirement party.

The 1990s: a time of change - when 3 women work together

Sense Scotland and Gill Morbey

7: Gill Morbey

In the 1950s there was a Rubella epidemic which left many children whose mothers had been in contact with Rubella, having a number of disabilities, Congenital Rubella Syndrome (CRS). These included deafness, deafblindness, physical disabilities, and learning disabilities, amongst others. Ten families came together to fight for their children who had Congenital Rubella Syndrome. Soon they began to campaign for help. In the 1960s the Rubella epidemic continued, and a growing band of families was affected. The National Deaf-Blind and Rubella Association was formed. In 1965 Jessica Hills became the chairperson and remained so for a number of years, taking the national organisation to national prominence which brought great benefit to congenitally deafblind people. As Rubella immunisation began, epidemics slowly became a thing of the past, but the challenges for deafblind people and their families remained ever present. Their campaign was for the education authorities to recognise the special needs of deafblind children.

In 1985, Sense Scotland formalised as a charity and appointed its first staff member, Gill Morbey, who, as the parent of a deafblind child, was well aware of the difficulties parents faced in trying to get services for their children. A year later the office and charity shop were opened in Glasgow. And in 1987 the Overbridge Continuing Education Centre opened in Glasgow, and Sense Scotland's income topped £1m for the first time. In 1989 Children in Need awarded Sense Scotland £300,000 for a new family resource centre. In the same year, HRH The Princess Royal became Sense Scotland's new patron.

In the 1990s the government started a programme of closing long-stay hospitals as a result of the policy of Care in the Community, and Sense Scotland began to provide more housing for the people discharged from long-stay hospitals. By 1999, Sense Scotland had 73 group homes across the UK providing supported housing and further education to 314 deafblind people.

In 1989 Deafblind UK opened an office at Barrowfield Deaf-blind Complex. Just over a year later, in 1991, the Sense Scotland Glasgow Family Resource Centre was opened by HRH Princess Anne, and Dorrie Moore, who is introduced below, attended to represent Deafblind Scotland as a deafblind adult while I served as her guide/communicator. For the first time there was representation for deafblind people of all ages, including those with congenital deafblindness and those with acquired deafblindness. The 2 organisations served people right across the age ranges.

In 1999, Sense Scotland and Deafblind Scotland jointly lobbied the new Scottish Parliament when a joint "Yes to Access" campaign was mounted soon after the parliament opened that year. This campaign sowed the seeds for the issuing of Section 7 Guidance in England and Wales in 2001. However, despite a long hard effort by both organisations to achieve a similar result in Scotland, this was not possible. The story of Section 7 Guidance is told in more detail in Chapter 14.

In 2010 Gill Morbey OBE, formerly chief executive of Sense Scotland became chief executive of Sense UK and in 2015 Sense celebrated its 60th anniversary by launching the "We All Need Friends" campaign.

Dorrie Moore (1922-2004)

8: Dorrie Moore

Dorrie was born on 31 January 1922 in the south of England and described herself as an Essex girl long before that term took on its current meaning. She loved Southend-on-Sea and, after moving to Scotland, regularly returned there for holidays with her husband John, who was a Scot. She used both British Sign Language (BSL) and Deafblind Manual to communicate with John and others. Dorrie had 2 daughters who communicated with their mum by pulling on her skirt, 2 pulls for someone at the door, 3 pulls for someone wanting to speak with her, and lots of rapid pulls for an emergency!

Dorrie became an active member of the NDBL and then became the organisation's divisional secretary for Scotland for 10 years. She spoke widely at conferences, training opportunities, and Deafblind UK (DBUK) rallies and conventions. Every few years a Deafblind Convention was held which was attended by people from all over the world – there was one held in Edinburgh in 1990 – and this enabled Dorrie and others to make friends from across the world. She also represented Scotland at DBUK national meetings.

On a more local basis she was secretary of the Rainbow Club which was run by a small dedicated group of volunteers led by Anne Patrick. They met on Monday nights, with people being picked up by bus from different areas in Glasgow and dropped off at Glasgow and West of Scotland Society for the Blind's premises in St George's Cross. For an hour and a half, they drank tea, played dominoes, and enjoyed communicating with each other using a whole range of communication methods. One assistant was provided, who accompanied each deafblind person from their front door and helped them safely onto the bus. For many of the 25 people who went along it was their main outing in the week.

Dorrie was also involved in a deafblind club held on a Friday in St Vincent's Centre for the Deaf. This was run by Glasgow Social Work Department staff and was a wonderful place for Social Work staff to learn about deafblindness, and it was also a great way to keep deafblind people informed about Social Work and other issues. Trainee social workers from all over Glasgow came to volunteer for an hour and they learned a great deal, including how to use Deafblind

Manual. They also learned that Dorrie could smell newly mown grass from hundreds of yards away, she knew when she was going over the Kingston bridge as she could smell the water, and she could identify people some distance away simply by their perfume or aftershave.

When the archdiocese and the Daughters of Charity of Saint Vincent de Paul succeeded in creating a housing complex in Glasgow which was specially adapted for deaf and deafblind people, one of Dorrie's dreams had come true. On its completion in 1989 she and John moved there. Dorrie led the campaign for the appointment of a Scottish Liaison Officer who could better support Scottish deafblind people. Soon after the Barrowfield Deaf-blind Complex opened in 1989, a part-time post was advertised and her efforts were rewarded when I was employed, 2 days per week, in September 1989. Dorrie had worked hard to bring about these advances.

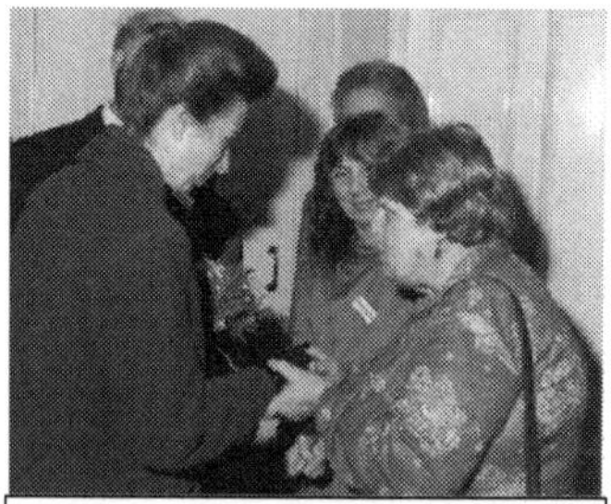

9: The opening of Sense Family Centre, 1991. HRH Princess Royal, Dorrie Moore, Drena O'Malley

As a fully deafblind lady for more than 30 years and Divisional Secretary for Scotland, she was a leading light in taking forwards the needs of deafblind people. Dorrie never missed an opportunity to promote deafblindness and was delighted to meet prominent figures, to communicate with them, to teach them how to use Deafblind Manual, to introduce them to deafblindness. As Divisional Secretary, she met

Archbishop Winning at the opening of the Barrowfield Complex, HRH The Princess Anne at the opening of the new Sense Scotland family resource centre in Glasgow, and Pope John Paul II during a trip to Italy. She also met television personalities Andy Cameron and Kaye Adams, and invariably charmed them. They were won over by her ready smile, and her sense of humour in the face of adversity.

Dorrie was particularly nervous in medical situations and was dedicated to ensuring that nurses learned Deafblind Manual, as deafblind people in a medical setting are particularly vulnerable and could be put at risk by lack of communication support. With the help of the Sister Cecilia and others from the order of the Daughters of Charity of Saint Vincent de Paul, Dorrie, over the years, taught thousands of nurses and other professionals Deafblind Manual. The gain for these professionals was really in meeting Dorrie and listening to her talk about her life, her fears, and her hopes. Part of her ongoing legacy is the improvement in the communication skills of nursing staff which deafblind people have benefitted from during the last 20 years. When I was in hospital in 2018 a nurse asked me about my work and, when I told her I had worked for Deafblind Scotland until earlier in the year, she remembered being taught Deafblind Manual by Dorrie as a student nurse, some 20 years previously, and could still remember the Deafblind Manual Alphabet.

However, there was another side to Dorrie. Her great fear was isolation and loneliness. She did not want to be alone, and she wanted to have communication all the time. I quickly came to understand that unless someone was using Deafblind Manual with her, nothing existed outside of herself. It is the normal state of being for those who are fully deafblind, with no sight and no hearing. Dorrie also suffered from Charles Bonnet Syndrome, which meant she experienced flashes of light in her head and she sometimes "saw" things, shadows, of people or animals, perhaps only a black outline. This sometimes went on for several hours, making concentration difficult and sleep often impossible.

She knew and talked about the fact that her mental health was fragile, that deafblindness caused her to be unsure of things, to check and re-check. She said that when she became deafblind she felt as if she somehow began to disappear, that people began to speak about her, rather than to her, and this made her fearful. She mostly appeared happy and laughing in public, unless it was a day when her fears had overtaken her, then her fearfulness was apparent.

Dorrie once described her life to me thus: "I live in a dark, silent cupboard with the door closed. People walk past, I can feel the vibration of their footsteps. Sometimes they open the door, and do Deafblind Manual on my hand. Then I know the world still exists." (from the Deafblind Scotland report, *Decade of Delay* (2005))

Dorrie and I worked closely together for 15 years. She always wanted a centre, a building, a place which was specially designed for deafblind people, by deafblind people, which belonged to them, a place of their own, which was designed to meet their needs. It is a matter of regret to me that she didn't see "Field of Dreams" become a reality in her lifetime.

I was privileged to be with her when she was ill, in hospital, and nearing the end of her life. I was manualling to her the words of her favourite hymn "All things bright and beautiful" and singing it at the same time. Others had left the room thinking, like me, she was tired, no longer holding her hand up, and no longer taking anything in. As I spelled out on her hand the chorus for the third time she quietly began to sing "All things wise and wonderful", at the right time and with the correct rhythm. Therein lay a huge lesson for me, one which I never forgot. Never assume you're not getting through.

Deafblind Scotland and Drena O'Malley

10: Drena O'Malley interpreting for Dorrie Moore

I replied to an advertisement for a part-time liaison officer with the NDBL in July 1989. I had been working with groups of parents and children in Royston Primary School, situated in, what was then, one of Glasgow's most deprived areas. Some of the mums had poor literacy skills and developing these skills was a priority. As a community we were also working to achieve the goal of having permanent accommodation for the group. And we were making progress; even more importantly it was the mums who were making that progress. And in the course of doing that, improving their own skills.

Working hands-on in an area of deprivation had taught me that solutions imposed on people, however well intentioned, rarely worked as well as those devised by the people themselves. We had worked hard in Royston to ensure the parents were listened to and supported to tackle their concerns, their way, to meet with those in positions of authority, to negotiate solutions and to implement them. When I read about the job in NDBL I could not imagine how deafblind people might ever be empowered to do the same. But I wanted to try.

11: Sarah Echlin and Sister Kay Hart outside Barrowfield Deaf-Blind Complex

When I met Dorrie and Richard James from head office at the interview I was fascinated by the tactile communication which flowed naturally between them and, in an hour, I was hooked. Dorrie taught me Deafblind Manual that day, we shared jokes, I was offered the post, and I started to work a few weeks later. My new office was the sleepover room for the staff working in the Barrowfield Deaf-blind Complex. They folded up their bed in the morning and I used that room as an office during the day for more than 4 years.

Richard James, and the then chief executive of NDBL, Ann Barnett, proved to be inspirational to work for. Richard believed that anyone could be Prime Minister – if they had enough appropriate support. And deafblind people didn't achieve their ambitions simply because they didn't have the necessary communication and guiding support they needed. Both of them were hands-on people who wanted the lives of Scottish deafblind people to improve. And both of them were committed to Dorrie, as I, too, quickly became.

Dorrie had ambitions – that the general public should know about deafblindness and should know how to communicate with deafblind people. She wanted deafblind people to have a fuller life. And she wanted to speak for herself, to give her opinion, to tell her story in her own words.

I quickly learned that the only way others will hear deafblind people speak for themselves is if sighted-hearing people make a conscious decision not to speak for them. It would have been easier to attend speaking opportunities on my own. But I sought opportunities where Dorrie could inform others about the best way to communicate with deafblind people and how to help them. She became a sought-after speaker on her favourite subject. And people remembered her long after she had spoken to them.

When I started in 1989, there were 66 members, spread throughout Scotland, whom I tried to visit on a regular basis, gathering information on their problems, needs, and desires, as well as those of their families. This number steadily grew as I travelled around the country, and it became clear that NDBL's initial idea to establish the liaison officer role in Scotland, as a way of meeting some of the need, had indeed created a huge list of needs far greater than one person could meet, or indeed even the UK organisation could meet. Ann Barnett agreed that any funds I could raise in Scotland could be spent in Scotland, so I was soon joined by Ellen Cattanach, part-time administrator, and a few months later by Wendy Forrest as Campaigns Officer. We were a small committed team taking on a huge challenge.

And in the early 1990s the relationship between Sense Scotland and the Scottish Office of NDBL was very important at a critical time. Gill Morbey and I worked together on a number of issues which affected both groups. Over the years we chose the issues where we could help one another, where working together would make a stronger case for the needs of deafblind people. And we worked separately for these 2 groups with very different needs when it would be more effective to do so. There was no time to waste as we uncovered so many different unmet needs in both groups – those with congenital deafblindness, and those with acquired deafblindness.

The Scottish office of NDBL spent the next 10 years trying to accomplish several things, one being to develop the membership, another being to develop a specialist guide/communicator service for deafblind people, and thirdly to raise funds to enable these things to happen.

The membership grew through the years from 66 to almost 800 in 2017. The guide/communicator service was much more of a challenge, as we had to create and develop a workforce, a profession to provide the service, and secure ongoing funding for that service. However, once a service was started in Glasgow, it grew. I had an aim to see deafblind people have a guide/communicator service, as a right, free at the point of use, in the same way as deaf people access a

BSL interpreting service. It is on record that between 2001 and 2013 the service grew from 17,000 hours of service in 2001 to 50,000 hours in 2013. The story of the guide/communicator service is worthy of its own chapter and is told in more detail in Chapter 11.

Deafblind people wanted to meet with each other, they wanted an input into, and to be involved in, running the organisation, without travelling to Peterborough. They wanted to pursue group activities. So, from early days, there was some interest in setting up a separate Scottish organisation. I saw the situation as being that deafblind people could do very little unless they had access to that vital communication and guiding support, so implementing a service was the priority. How deafblind people represented themselves is told in Chapter 9 about the evolution of the Scottish Advisory Group on Deafblindness (SAGOD) meetings. And how the new Scottish charity came about is detailed in Chapter 13.

I was committed to being led by deafblind people and I could not dampen their enthusiasm for more participation in their organisation. They wanted to speak for themselves and they wanted to be listened to, to influence outcomes at every level. The story of how deafblind people worked with a small staff team to influence what was happening in Scotland is told in Chapters 8 to 15.

The "Field of Dreams" story is detailed in Chapters 17 to 20, as it may be interesting not only to deafblind people but to others who face the daunting prospect of running a capital project for a new building. When I researched how to fundraise for capital projects, I could find little factual information based on lived experience, as most information was about the problems one might experience.

Patrick Murphy

Patrick Murphy was born sighted-hearing becoming deafblind as an adult. Patrick was a consultant on deafblindness for NDBL when I started in 1989 and had been so for several years. He was listed as a director of NDBL in 1993. As Chairman of the European Commission on Activities for the Deaf-Blind he was involved in the development of the definition of deafblindness, a slightly adapted version of which remains in use today:

> "A person is Deaf-Blind when he/she has a severe degree of combined visual and auditory impairment resulting in extreme communication, information and mobility problems
>
> Deaf-blindness is a handicap presenting other difficulties than those caused by blindness or deafness alone
>
> Accordingly, a deaf-blind person needs special facilities to overcome these difficulties in daily living, and in education, work and social activities"

12: Patrick Murphy

He was heavily involved with the World Blind Union, and a skilled Braille user who communicated with other Braille users across the world.

He was chairperson of a major 7-day conference for deafblind people in September 1991 at Cramond Campus, Moray House College, Edinburgh. Over 200 deafblind people and communicators from countries including Japan, Italy, America, England, Ireland, France, Denmark, Finland, and Norway attended the conference which had more spoken, written, and signed languages used over the 7-day period than any other, in the UK, before or since.

The convention was opened by Lady Strathmore, long-term supporter of Sense Scotland who was invited to Sense Scotland through Dr John Tulloch and his wife Sheena; John was the first chairperson. The keynote address was delivered by James Anderson, a governor of Jordanstown School, a deaf school in Northern Ireland which admitted deafblind people. Mornings for the rest of the week were spent in workshops, many led by deafblind people themselves. These included speakers Emlyn Cassam, Director of Social Services, Norwich, Dottie Entwhistle from NDBL, and a rep from the American organisation AADB speaking on "The Road to Success". Doug Alker Head of Regional Services RNID, Dottie Entwhistle, and Mrs White spoke on "Deaf-Blind Services – what is available, what is needed". Yvonne Maquardi, US young deaf achiever of the year, spoke on "Equal Rights and Choices".

On the Thursday morning of that week a deafblind rally was arranged. At that time NDBL arranged this event each year and deafblind people from all parts of the UK gathered to socialise. So, on that Thursday, numbers attending swelled when even more people from Scotland joined the international group.

The afternoons and evenings were taken up with outings and entertainment. Included in the list was a Jacobean Banquet, a walk around Cramond, a ceilidh, a trip to Ingleston market, an open-top bus trip around Edinburgh, a visit to Hopetoun House, and trips to Butterfly World, the Dry Ski Slope, Edinburgh Zoo, Holyrood House, the Royal Museum, Inchcolm Island, St Andrews, Loch Lomond and Callander, Edinburgh Castle, New Lanark, the Whisky Heritage Centre, the Royal Botanic Gardens, Dalmeny House, and a canal trip, to name a selection of them.

Patrick wrote poetry and in the following poem describes deafblindness thus:

Sharing

My world is dark and silent:
it's like this year by year
For I can see no image,
and neither can I hear
But don't misunderstand,
I could 'see' and 'hear' before,
Can picture what the world is like;
my memory is a store.
This is a great advantage,
and helps me to live on,
To use my other senses,
to help me get things done.
I've seen both birds and insects,
and many kinds of trees,
Seen flowers in the Autumn,
dance briskly in the breeze.
I'll 'see' the clouds and sunshine,
I'll 'hear the sounds of song'

Which forms th'intangible link
with the busy happy throng.
I've seen all kinds of creatures,
heard folk in play and strife
Seen sad and joyful dramas,
the things that make up life.
I now can use my fingers
to take the place of sight
And often feel vibrations
that tell I've done things right.
This is compensation
for the loss of sight and sound,
But it is still much better
when one with sight is round.
I spill things without knowing,
and maybe leave a stain
My sighted friends will tell me
and make the matter plain
Adapted aids and gadgets
are useful in my days
And serve to make life easier
in many little ways
But still I look most forward
to times when Lynne will come
For then I feel a presence,
a spirit in my home
Lynne likes to drink my coffee
and have a little chat
And then she is a whirlwind
that flies about my flat
At times I can't find something
and think a fairy's been
But realise it's more likely
to have been simply Lynne
A deafblind person's problem

is to keep an active mind
Is much relieved by good friends
who'll pop in, and are kind.
We have some fun and laughter
and many points are aired
And both, I think, are better
for jokes and problems shared
Another friend will visit,
and so much pleasure brings
She's like a ray of sunshine,
a pixie without wings
Its best if one can mostly
forget one is deafblind
And live like other people,
and share in life, I find
So spend time with one another,
and stimulate your wit
You'll find it satisfying,
and both will benefit.

Father Cyril Axelrod

13: Fr Cyril Axelrod

Father Cyril Axelrod was born on 24 February 1942, in South Africa to Jewish parents. His paternal grandfather was a Rabbi, his parents, for whom, English was very much a second language, spoke Yiddish. He was a gentle, quiet baby, who was slow to walk, possibly due to balance problems. His deafness was diagnosed at 3 years of age, which was a body blow to his parents who were then determined to find the best possible education for him. However, there was no suitable Jewish school for the deaf, and after much deliberation his parents reluctantly agreed that Cyril should attend St Vincent's School for the Deaf in Johannesburg. The parents were delighted when, in time, the school agreed to ensure their son learned about the "God of Israel" at school. Father Cyril explained in his book *And the Journey Begins*, "At the time, parents were not encouraged to use sign language with their deaf children, as lipreading and speech were the preferred methods. As an adult, my pastoral work would teach me how much some deaf people have suffered as a result of this."

As he grew into a young man he was drawn more and more to the Catholic faith, and finally in 1970 he was ordained as a priest in Johannesburg. His Jewish family could not accept his becoming a priest and he had little contact with them for several years. He committed his life to serving deaf people and over the years he did this in South Africa, America, South East Asia, and Europe. Father Cyril began his ministry in South Africa with deaf and deafblind people who used 8 indigenous sign languages. Defying apartheid, he established a multi-racial school for deaf children in Soweto, a hostel for deaf homeless people in Pretoria, and an employment centre in Cape Town. He helped to have schools, community centres, and homes built for deaf people as well as seeking to educate them, whenever he found them, all across the world.

In 1980 he went to the USA, visiting 27 states, and during this visit he went to see an ophthalmologist who confirmed that he had Retinitis Pigmentosa and was going to lose his sight, and therefore become deafblind due to Usher Syndrome. He knew at that point that he would become deafblind, that the time when he could do God's work was incredibly limited, and that he must therefore get on with it. He wanted to work with deaf people in South East Asia and finally he arranged to spend time in Macau where there were no services for deaf people. He spent time with Buddhist monks there and formed a strong relationship with them. Father Cyril could see more similarities than differences between the main religions, and concluded that they could all gain by learning from each other.

His 12 years in Macau were hugely productive and resulted in his being awarded a First Class Social Merit Medal by the World Federation of the Deaf for his work on the human rights of deaf people. However, by this time his visual field amounted to only 3%, and he had no sight at all in the dark. He had a whitish fog over both eyes like veils and his three-dimensional vision was distorted. This loss of his sight caused him to come to the UK in 2000 where, in his book *And the Journey Begins*, he described how he experienced periods of anguish, confusion, and frustration as he struggled to understand why "God had brought me to an unfamiliar country where everything is completely new to me. Now I was only seen as a deafblind man." He found that although he was using Hands-on Signing, some people in England withdrew from him when they realised he couldn't see sign. Father Cyril said "I felt I was leaving my community, as I became not deaf, but deaf-blind."

At this low point in a life totally devoted to service, Father Cyril was asked by Deafblind UK to be their Pastoral Support Development Coordinator to encourage pastoral care within churches. And then he received news that Gallaudet University, in Washington DC, had awarded him an honorary doctorate. This recognition could not have come at a better time as "it restored my belief that nothing could take my life's work away from me". On the day the award was presented he was overwhelmed by the experience of a standing ovation from the Gallaudet University audience and felt uplifted on his journey back to England that his work now was to serve deafblind people.

Since Father Cyril lost his sight, he has with new vigour sought to "help others see that, with the right assistance, deafblind people can take control of their own lives, their own decisions, and their own roles". Also to help sighted-hearing people see that "the really rewarding challenge is to see how a deafblind person, with assistance, fulfil their own hopes and aspirations, and make their own decisions, at a deeper level of independence".

Over the years Father Cyril has been a regular visitor to Scotland, and always finds time to meet with deafblind people, and give personal assistance where needed. His most recent visit was in November 2018. His training can really enlighten the most experienced guide/communicator as to how they might work with deafblind people. In July 2006 he joined us at Deafblind Scotland's annual forum on deafblindness and spoke about his journey to becoming a deafblind person. At a training session for guide/communicators in Glasgow 2 years later, he challenged them all to examine if they focussed on enabling deafblind people to make decisions for themselves on any course of action, or if they inadvertently or otherwise enabled deafblind people to make the expected decision. He used his own experience of achieving funding for a regular guide/communicator service to illustrate how it might be done. His ability to question, to challenge constructively, is a very effective tool in training and his sessions are always in demand.

Apart from receiving a number of international awards, Father Cyril has been privileged to meet 3 popes. In 2014 he received an OBE from the Queen in recognition of the help he gave to the Hong Kong Society for the Blind to set up services for deafblind people including training courses and counselling.

He is a qualified aromatherapist, and he has recently worked with 2 professional artists to learn about painting. He has celebrated his Golden Jubilee in the priesthood by publishing a book of paintings titled "Light in Silent Darkness". All of his painting is done using tactile means.

Danny Delcambre

14: Danny Delcambre, 1999

Danny was born in Louisiana, USA, in 1962, was deaf from birth and describes himself as Cajun. He began to lose his sight in his teens, a slow, gradual process due to Retinitis Pigmentosa. Danny has Usher Syndrome. There is a high incidence of Usher Syndrome within the Cajun population. He attended a state school for the deaf from the age of 5 until he was 20. His first job was washing tables in McDonald's. After 5 years he was promoted to try cooking. He then went to trade school and learned to become an accountant. He required an interpreter to study there, and in the end, his mother interpreted for him. This led to a job for 3 years in a warehouse which provided food to offshore workers. However, after those 3 years, he was laid off, and remained unemployed for 2 years.

Danny's Cajun tenacity then came to the fore when a friend suggested he move to Seattle where facilities for deafblind people were very good. So, he did. However, the streets of Seattle were not quite paved with gold, and he found he couldn't get a job. One of the businesses he applied to was Boeing, who suggested he attend a course at a local college. While there he really enjoyed the food and found out it was made by culinary students. At this point he decided to change his course and enrolled in a culinary arts course. He was awarded 6 scholarships, so he could afford to use an interpreter, and he immediately accepted an internship with a famous Cajun chef and then undertook a course in research and marketing, and used this to interview restaurant owners, gaining valuable information about running a restaurant. After graduation, however, he watched as hearing students were offered chef-type roles, but he was offered only dishwashing jobs.

He decided to set up his own business and took out a bank loan to do so, which took him 6 years to repay. He started his own restaurant "Rajin Cajun" and employed – against all advice – 3 deaf employees and 3 hearing employees who could sign.

Danny came to Scotland in 1999 to speak at Deafblind UK Scottish office's 8th annual forum on deafblindness (for more information on Forums see Chapter 9). Danny then spent the weekend speaking at the first ever Scottish conference on Usher Syndrome, held at Dudhope Castle, University of Abertay. He spoke about his Rajin Cajun restaurant and the success it had become after 9 years. How financially it had worked out even though he had not always taken on board the professional advice he had been given. He also spoke about the constant adaptations he needed to make to his communication in order to remain in contact with others. When he spoke at the Usher Syndrome Conference, he could still see enough to look at an interpreter carefully placed straight ahead of him. He was inspirational to the 40 people with Usher Syndrome who had the opportunity to meet him over the weekend.

Danny received a number of awards over the years, including the President's Award for Outstanding Small Employer of the year. He met President Clinton when he visited his restaurant to sample Danny's Cajun cooking. He became an internationally acclaimed inspirational speaker as well as vice president of Washington State Deaf-Blind Citizens, and a board member of other organisations.

In more recent years he has sold his restaurant. His sight is now almost totally gone. However, he has developed a new skill creating paintings of birds in his garden, using a telescope to see them with the little remaining central vision he has.

Stephen Joyce

15: Stephen Joyce

Stephen was born in 1973, to sighted-hearing parents to whom it was soon obvious that he might have a hearing problem. They were told he was too young to be tested and they were being over-anxious. They persevered, and some time later he was confirmed as being deaf. He received weekly visits from teachers of the deaf, which were fun and he enjoyed them. He started Ewing school aged 2½, travelling daily by minibus. His parents learned Cued speech hoping this would help with his spoken language as signing was not allowed in school. It didn't appear to help too much, but aural education it was, so they persevered.

By the time he was 7 it was noticed that he was often falling off his bike when riding from dark areas into bright areas, and a sight test was arranged, but nothing was found. He attended St John's Catholic School for the Deaf (colloquially known as Boston Spa). By the time he was 10 years old, he was diagnosed with Usher Syndrome, which was a shock to his parents and to the professionals previously involved. Stephen just got on with things living a normal life, with a few inevitable restrictions of course.

Football was his main sporting love. He was an avid supporter of Nottingham Forest, and continues to be to this day. When he realised he couldn't play football, he adapted by taking up running which he continues to do even although he is now registered blind. He went on to college and university and achieved a BSc (Hons) Information Systems from Derby University. He regularly pays tribute to the part played by good communication support services available to all deaf students at Derby.

Towards the end of his degree he saw a new post advertised at Deafblind Scotland for a project coordinator of their Usher Syndrome Project. He applied, was interviewed, and was successful. He began that 3-year project in1997 creating a whole new awareness of Usher Syndrome across the NHS, Social Work, and the Deaf community in Scotland. This was a vital project which was funded by the National Lottery Charities Board, and, in the end, Stephen succeeded in identifying 57 people with Usher Syndrome across Scotland. Considering the difficulties with communication that Usher Syndrome causes this is an amazing number and each one represents a different journey for that individual. He also ensured there was regular news about the project in every local paper, radio station, Social Work department, doctor's surgery, hospital, and school for the deaf, with 6000 leaflets being distributed across Scotland.

He was instrumental in bringing about the first ever Usher Syndrome Conference in Dundee. Stephen welcomed Danny Delcambre from Seattle as the main speaker. Of the large group of people who have Usher Syndrome and who met that weekend, many remain in contact with one another.

Stephen quickly became a sought-after speaker and a great representative for deafblind people. He embodied the ethos of the Scottish organisation which was very much that deafblind people should speak for themselves. The truth was simple, they were much more effective when they demonstrated that they can present as well as any sighted-hearing person, given the right communication support. This was never better evidenced than when Stephen played a pivotal role in meetings with Greater Glasgow NHS Board (GGNHSB) when he recounted his own experience in medical situations when he didn't have a BSL interpreter or a guide/communicator. The health professionals could then more easily understand the problem and this undoubtedly played a vital part in Deafblind Scotland being able to negotiate GGNHSB funding a guide/communicator service for deafblind people when in medical settings.

He went on to become Training Manager, training 500 people annually in British Sign Language, Communicating and Guiding with Deafblind People, Deafblind Manual, Hands-on Signing, and in computing skills. His clients included Deafblind Scotland staff, ScotRail, Police Scotland, NHS staff, Scottish Ambulance, Scottish Fire and Rescue, Social Work departments, and BBC Scotland, as well as the general public from all across Scotland. He taught classes in Aberdeen, Edinburgh, Dundee, as well as in Glasgow and in the centre in Lenzie. He was a Finalist in Signature's Teacher of the Year award, and an SQA nominee for Teacher of the Year. He was also an Olympic torch-bearer during London 2012 and carried the torch through the streets of Larbert ensuring several deafblind people who were in the crowd could touch it as it passed.

He never lost his love of football, running, or the great outdoors and became an enthusiastic fundraiser for Deafblind Scotland, particularly for the "Field of Dreams". He also regularly fundraised for ongoing activities for deafblind people, his biggest challenge being the climbing of Mount Kilimanjaro when he was accompanied by interpreter Jim Lee and ex-soldier Jim Harley. After a gruelling climb over many days, he insisted on finishing the final few hundred yards to the summit, in the dark, unaccompanied and this picture was taken at the top. It was an inspiring achievement for deafblind people and all concerned.

16: Jim Harley, Stephen Joyce, Jim Lee on the summit of Mt Kilimanjaro, 2008

Bob Nolan

17: Bob and Louise Nolan, Olympic Torch relay in Banchory, 2012

Bob was born in 1957, the eldest of 3 children and the only one with a hearing loss, which was diagnosed when he was 3 years old. Up to that point Bob was bilingual (his mum was Dutch) but the diagnosis prompted the decision to focus on English as it was thought it would be tough enough learning just one spoken language. Bob was fortunate that most of his hearing loss was in the higher frequencies which meant he could follow speech reasonably well in quiet surroundings and his own speech was relatively clear.

For 10 years he wore the old-fashioned body aid except when he was playing football, which was most of the time! Bob was the first deaf house captain at his primary school; quite an achievement for a boy who relied on lip-reading to know what the teacher was saying. However, his love of reading and his good command of English ensured success when he went to Mary Hare Grammar School for the deaf in Berkshire. Bob was a resilient character even at 13 and that resilience stood him in good stead as he began to realise he had a problem with his vision. This became obvious to him because he couldn't instantly see the football which had been passed to his feet. Indeed all sport became difficult, even cross country running. Losing access to playing football caused a real sense of loss.

However, a helpful French exchange student taught him 3 chords on his mum's guitar and, in his final year at school in 1975, he started a band with 2 of his friends. And Lumpy Custard was born. The band progressed to playing regular live gigs on Saturday nights in the school and later they appeared on BBC's Pebble Mill at One, TV South, and at the Royal Albert Hall for a celebration of music for the deaf. Back at school the enthusiasm of even profoundly deaf pupils for dancing to the band did not go unnoticed and Mary Hare developed a successful music curriculum, which continues to the present day.

University meant further adjustment as he was once again the only deaf person. As there were no note takers in the 1970s, Bob would listen and lip-read lectures and copy his friends' notes afterwards and he became very adept at reading poor handwriting!

Armed with a geography degree Bob quickly discovered he would not be able to follow his chosen career in secondary teaching because of his deafness so he took a gap year hitchhiking around the world instead. He saw many of the marvellous sights he had covered in his studies, not least Ayers Rock, the Grand Canyon. the Rockies, and Hawaii's volcanoes.

When he returned home 13 months later he began work as a trainee accountant in Wakefield, and within weeks saw an ophthalmologist for the very first time. He was told he had Retinitis Pigmentosa, and in tandem with his deafness this was Usher Syndrome. At that appointment he was informed that he would be fully blind in 5 years. His life plans had to change. He opted for a career in IT where he thought his worsening sight might be less of a hindrance. He joined Shell as a computer programmer months later, but said nothing about his impending blindness and only admitted to his deafness at final interview. In the meantime, he married his deaf sweetheart Louise and they moved to London in 1984.

After 8 years in IT he moved to Shell in Aberdeen, where he remained for the rest of his Shell career. While his sight continued to deteriorate, he never made an issue of it. He knew every inch of the Shell building and remained fiercely independent. His colleagues only began to realise the extent of his dual sensory loss when work took them outside of the familiar surroundings of the office.

In 1998 he attended an Usher Syndrome Roadshow in Aberdeen hosted by Stephen Joyce from Deafblind UK's Scottish office and realised there were organisations who could offer support. I met Bob soon after and immediately saw the potential he had to be an example to other deafblind people who had dreams and ambitions.

Although we didn't know it at the time, for years we would work in partnership to improve the lives of deafblind people in Scotland. We would enable them to play a greater part in decision-making within the organisation and further afield. We shared a similar outlook and were able to work effectively together for a very special group of people. Bob became a member of the organisation and in time joined the Management Steering Group which would eventually decide on separation from Deafblind UK and setting up a separate Scottish charity in 2001.

Bob was elected the first chairperson of the new organisation, Deafblind Scotland, and worked hard to involve deafblind people at every stage of building the organisation. Bob was very aware, as I was, that he was not a typical deafblind person and said to me more than once, "I never fail to appreciate how fortunate I am compared to many deafblind people." But that also meant he had experience, for example in his working life, which other deafblind people didn't have, and which was very useful to a small charity. However, he also had other commitments in his life – Shell UK, where he led a Pan-European Team of 70 people, not to mention his wife and 3 children. He was committed to the idea of a member-led organisation, knowing how frustrated he would be if he weren't able to contribute. He was a workaholic, possibly because he knew how much longer it could take for him to access all the information he needed, compared to others.

But as noted earlier Bob was resilient and never gave up on the idea of participating in sport. He took up running and swimming as ways to keep fit. Other deafblind people looked at Bob and wondered "How does he do it?" He continued to run on paths he knew, but had his fair share of accidents and injuries.

He became a lead on Disability Awareness within Shell and this was a role he enjoyed. In this role he spoke on disability all over Europe, in Nigeria, Egypt, India, Australia, and Malaysia, and to the Houses of Parliament in 2011. Bob represented Shell at the "2016 City for the Future" Disability Conference in Cairo where he was a guest of the Egyptian President and met some truly inspirational people there who've made a real difference in all walks of life and cultures.

Bob ran 3 Edinburgh marathons raising over £6000 for Deafblind Scotland general funds. Then, when the "Field of Dreams" piece of land became available in 2007, Bob threw himself into fundraising for the monies needed to purchase the land. He tried tandem cycling with his wife Louise, and he loved it. That became a major way for Bob and Louise to raise funds over a 5-year period (see Chapter 19 for more). There was a small dedicated group of deafblind people who, possibly inspired by Bob's example, committed to raising funds for the new building. They remained totally committed for a period of 10 years to getting that piece of land, the funds needed, the planning permission to build, and the building completed.

Hammy and I supported Bob and Louise on all their rides, together with friends of Bob's from all over UK who were keen supporters of his fundraising efforts. I was left in awe of this couple's determination. Louise is a small, slim woman who cycled on the front of a tandem for up to 90 miles per day, seeming to survive on only hot chocolate and yoghurt. Bob was the powerhouse at the back. I often drove the van while Hammy cycled with them. To watch them struggle up some of Scotland's highest hills in the pouring rain was a humbling experience, and one which undoubtedly helped me to maintain my commitment.

In 2012 Bob was delighted to carry the Olympic Torch in Banchory. This meant 2 deafblind people got to carry the Olympic torch in Scotland which gave deafblind members a reason to be proud.

In 2016 Bob retired from a long career at Shell and in 2017 moved back to England to be closer to his family. Bob was quickly recruited by DBUK as a trustee and on 1 April 2018 became their chairperson in their 90th year. Bob continued to chair Deafblind Scotland until 2019. The 2 organisations have historically always worked closely together and now share a Memorandum of Understanding.

In 2017 Bob was delighted to see the building completed and to welcome HRH The Princess Royal to open the "Field of Dreams" new National Training and Development Centre for deafblind people, a fitting end to a 10 year commitment.

To celebrate the 90th anniversary of the inception of the NDBL, Bob attempted the Three Peaks Tandem challenge with his long-suffering wife Louise and some very good friends. Together they climbed Ben Nevis, Scafell Pike, and Snowdon and cycled the 483 miles in between in 5 days raising a further £6500 for the 2 charities. It continued as a good year when Bob received the Unsung Hero Award at the Deaf Sports Personality of the Year dinner. He maintained that his wife Louise should really have won it. Finally, he was recognised by OSCR when he received their 2018 Terrific Trustee Award.

Bob enjoys playing guitar in a local band called Crowsfeet and with only him and Louise now in the house he finally has time to practise. He also enjoys swimming in the local open-air pool, cycling, running, hillwalking with the Sheffield Blind Walking Group, and he recently became a befriender in his local village. As his wife Louise says, “Robert has only retired from paid work!”

He continues to lead by example, creating awareness of deafblindness wherever he goes. He is a prolific and inspirational speaker and has become an ambassador for the Sheffield Royal Society for the Blind, the closest society to where he now lives. He is not only Chairperson but also a befriender for DBUK and is delighted to meet members as part of both roles. He maintains his commitment to deafblind people being at the forefront of a deafblind organisation.

John Whitfield

18: John Whitfield

John was born in Nevern, Wales, in 1958, the second child of hearing parents, and was diagnosed as hearing impaired at the age of 3; his brother was diagnosed at the same time, aged 7. Both wore body-worn hearing aids at school – well at least when they were allowed to as they were told to remove them for sporting activities and for photographs apparently! John loved sports, particularly rugby and swimming. When he grew up he developed an interest in riding motorbikes which became a compulsion and later got in the way of his education. Then, in his early twenties, having just started college John had just one motorbike accident too many and realised he was struggling with his sight. He was referred to an ophthalmologist who told him "You have Usher type 2, and you will be totally blind by the age of 40 and there is nothing we can do."

John went through a difficult period, gave up his college course, and really rebelled against everything. But then he was seen by another ophthalmologist who reassured him that those people diagnosed with Usher type 2 can live until their eighties with some useful central vision. John re-joined his college course, completed his degree in horticulture, and then moved to Scotland where he met his wife.

He also met me when I turned up unannounced at his home to visit one day. John brushed me and my offers of help aside, saying he did not need help, but I left him saying "When the time comes we will be there for you." I knew his resilience was sustaining him, together with the support of his wife Becky.

Some years later we met again when John was working on his dissertation for a master's degree in psychology, and he asked to interview deafblind members as part of his dissertation. From there on he became committed to working to help deafblind people reach their potential. This he did in several roles at Deafblind Scotland over 15 years and he and I became firm friends as I worked to persuade him to develop communication skills, encouraging him to learn Deafblind Manual, and, in time, sign language, all as sensible preparation for a future where a range of communication skills might be needed.

John became involved in the steering group seeking to set up a separate Scottish charity in 1999, while completing his MA (Hons) psychology degree – the first deafblind person in Scotland to achieve a degree. When the new charity became a reality in 2001, he took up a role working with deafblind people and has continued to do so until this day, working on various projects, all of which have sought to enable deafblind people to improve their quality of life. Meantime he found the stamina to undertake the Diploma in Deafblind Studies, and in 2008 became the first deafblind person to achieve the qualification in Scotland.

Amongst various roles within the organisation, John was project manager of the "Touching Lives" project, the winning project of the BBC/BLF Primetime competition in 2008. Over 3 years the project managed to involve 5000 schoolchildren in learning about deafblindness, all taught by deafblind people who had been specially trained by John. The project also introduced to deafblind awareness almost 2000 adults in organisations, social services, health settings, and rotary clubs. Every deafblind person who became a trainer and took part in the project benefitted from the project, reporting that their confidence and ability to interact with others in their community had greatly improved.

John became involved in training with Stephen and almost immediately seriously committed to learning sign language, something I had been trying to persuade him to do for some time, and for his own benefit. It is worth noting that most people I taught Deafblind Manual to over the years learned the skill for someone else's benefit, and not their own. He trained professional groups in deafblind awareness and now trains guide/communicators and others as well as representing the organisation in various roles. He has become the proud owner of guide dog Peat, and now has a British Sign Language qualification. He has also become a BSL assessor at that level.

Like Stephen and Bob, as well as Michael (mentioned below), he is a great lover of the outdoors and has been a stalwart fundraiser for the "Field of Dreams" project, over the years trekking in various challenging places, raising funds for "Field of Dreams" (for more information see Chapter 19).

So much for the ophthalmologist's forecast!

Irene Birse

When I first met Irene in 1994 she was a very angry lady. She was angry with the ophthalmologist who had just informed her that she must stop driving; angry with her GP who knew little or nothing about Usher Syndrome; angry with those in her everyday life who knew about her sight problem but still expected her to have 20:20 vision; she was angry with those who expected too much of her and just as angry with those who expected too little. She was deeply angry with her husband, her soulmate, who had died at the ripe old age of 38 leaving her on her own to bring up 2 young children, aged 12 and 9, which Irene described to me as "a very bad age to lose a daddy". And I came into her life because she had just recently been diagnosed with Usher Syndrome.

19: Irene Birse taken at a SAGOD meeting 1997

Every day was a momentous struggle to cope. She was employed caring for others at a time when she could barely care for herself and her children and her house. The prospect of being unemployed at that moment was the final blow and she fought to keep her job as a carer. Until the day she walked into an open cupboard door in a client's house once too often, and she and her employer agreed she could indeed be a danger to others as well as herself. She gave up driving, she gave up her family home in an idyllic little village, and moved to the comparative metropolis of Montrose.

Irene at that time needed information about Usher Syndrome, but in small amounts and at the right moment. She needed communication support, but not always. She needed others to recognise and allow for her hearing and visual loss, but not to focus on them. She needed to meet others who had Usher Syndrome, but only when she was ready. It took time for Irene to come to terms with not being able to drive, having to rely on her mother for help with the children, not being able to do simple things for herself. She had good friends who knew she was fiercely independent and who, whenever possible, let her find her own way through several very difficult years, supporting without ever taking control.

The Care sector's loss was, however, Deafblind Scotland's gain. Irene had already begun a number of campaigns in her local area, some of them personal crusades, for example to remove pavement furniture which caused her to fall over, to get access for deafblind people to better information services on trains, her main method of transport, and to get individuals to listen to what deafblind people say for themselves. She believed that if deafblind people said nothing to the authorities, things would never improve. Indeed it was their duty to represent their needs, make suggestions for improvements, and campaign for change.

Deafblind adults can sometimes display signs of defeatism, a learned acceptance of being a victim of discrimination, show apathy towards any kind of self-representation, and believe they personally are pretty powerless to affect their life's journey. This sentence could not be used to describe Irene at any point in the time I have known her. When she became involved with Deafblind UK's Scottish office she was an inspiration to others. When the idea of a Scottish Advisory Group on Deafblindness was first mentioned, that it would be a forum for members, and would be held in different towns and cities across Scotland, she immediately wanted to arrange one in Dundee.

She chaired the first SAGOD meeting in Kirkintilloch in October 1997, quite a challenge for any deafblind person. She encouraged deafblind people that this was their opportunity to speak their minds, make suggestions, represent their needs. And this approach became the watchword for SAGOD over the years, earning it the reputation of being truly representative of deafblind people's views. She re-enforced to the sighted-hearing professionals and politicians who had been invited along to the meeting that their privilege in this meeting should be to listen to views of deafblind people and to relish the opportunity to interact on a personal basis with them, with the support of a guide/communicator when necessary.

While she was championing the needs and rights of deafblind people she was dealt yet another blow in her personal life when her son Darren tragically died aged 36. Irene's daughter Diane, and 2 granddaughters, Kymberley and Chloe, saw her through a dark period and she threw herself into her work for Deafblind Scotland.

When the subject of greater representation for deafblind people in the governance of Deafblind UK, particularly in Scotland, became a standing agenda item at SAGOD meetings, Irene served on the Management Steering Group which sought a path to achieve this. And when that ambition was finally achieved in 2001 by setting up a separate charity, Deafblind Scotland, Irene joined in the "Hands around Scotland" celebration. She transported the flag in a 3-wheeled vintage laundry van she had acquired from Montrose up the coastal path to Aberdeen, delivering it to her deafblind friend George Simpson, who took it on a flight to Shetland. She was elected on to the newly established board of directors as vice-chair to Bob Nolan. They worked together to see the organisation through all the early days ensuring deafblindness was always on the agenda at all levels of government, and that deafblind people represented themselves at every opportunity. Irene served on the board until 2009.

In 2001 she applied for a DBUK Millennium Award to purchase a computer and other equipment to allow her to write a book about her journey through life with Usher Syndrome. Her application was successful and she spent the next 2 years working on a book. She galvanised many other deafblind people into writing about their adventures with Usher Syndrome for the book, Angus College into supporting her technically, David Whyte into providing the graphics, and myself into being a mentor, and writing a chapter about Usher Syndrome. And then she added some of her own stories which were almost always funny. Her book *Usher and US* was published in 2004. While some stories were rightly about all the difficulties those with Usher Syndrome face, many were inevitably humorous in nature, and served to show that having a sense of humour was a useful coping strategy for the strange things which can happen to people who have Usher Syndrome.

Twenty years later her sense of humour remains intact and she often uses it to support others in a similar situation to her own. She knows the difficulties. She also knows the possibilities and opportunities and how to use them to advantage.

Irene requested the following quote be included:

> "You made our lives bearable with your enthusiasm and encouragement to be independent. You built up DbS so we got to know each other and stopped being in isolation. You encouraged us to do things for ourselves, represent ourselves, take responsibility for our lives. I had forgotten how angry I was. How my life has changed from that time. I think my story could have been very different, very sad. Thank you for showing me there is life after an Usher Syndrome diagnosis."

Michael Anderson

20: Michael Anderson

Michael was born in Surrey in 1941. His mother noticed he didn't react to noise and he was later diagnosed as hearing impaired. At age 5 he was given a hearing aid which he carried in a leather bag, with wires coming from it, and he often got tangled in these wires. He attended a number of primary schools in England before the family moved to Glasgow where he met Miss Falconer, a teacher at his school, who took an interest in him and helped him catch up with the education he had missed. He was 2 years behind his age group. In the end he went to a senior secondary and in 1954 his visual impairment was diagnosed as Retinitis Pigmentosa (RP) because it was noted he was always bumping into things. He completed his 5th year at school, after which he went on a year-long practical farming course. As he later progressed through college on a National Diploma course it became apparent that a career in dairy farming was not going to be possible due to his dual sensory loss.

He found a post in book-keeping on a landed estate which meant he was at least working in the countryside. He then progressed to working for the Agricultural Council, and was placed at Edinburgh University, where he became a statistician.

He met his wife Betty in 1968 and they married a year later, and went on to live in Edinburgh for several years. Betty persuaded Michael to see a geneticist in the Western General Infirmary where he was asked 2 questions the answers to which immediately led to a suggestion that he had Usher Syndrome. He was aged 29. He was registered blind when he was 33 years old. Three years later he took early retirement at 37. He and Betty moved to Berwickshire with their 2 children, fulfilling Michael's ambition to live in the country. And their third child Ian was born there.

Life was idyllic for a year or 2 until Michael succumbed to depression, a condition from which he has since occasionally suffered.

In May 1997 Michael was referred to Deafblind UK's Scottish office and I visited him in Duns. It was obvious from that first visit that as well as Michael gaining from being involved with Deafblind Scotland, his skills could be invaluable, and he had a lot to offer this developing organisation.

He quickly got involved in helping set up the first meeting of the Scottish Advisory Group on Deafblindness in Kirkintilloch in November 1997 and was active from the beginning, contributing to discussions on what the group's aims should include. He saw this group as the means by which deafblind people could influence decisions. He was a great supporter of the aim (expanded in Chapter 9) that SAGOD should seek to "influence policy at every level – government, local authority, service-providers and society in general, and within Deafblind UK".

This group was a powerhouse for deafblind people in the years leading up to the setting up of a separate Scottish charity, and Michael faithfully produced a report from each meeting for the board of directors of NDBL. He was a supporter of the idea both of a separate Scottish charity where deafblind people could be more involved in the decision-making process and of the rights of deafblind people to speak for themselves.

Michael became a member of the management steering group charged with investigating and making recommendations to the SAGOD group about a new Scottish charity being formed. Between 1998 and 2000 he was a major player in bringing this change about. In addition, he represented deafblind people in Scotland on various Scottish Executive groups, including the "Sensing Progress" report group, and the "Sensory Impairment Action Plan" group, neither of which was designed to easily accommodate the needs of deafblind people, and he didn't miss a chance to remind them of that. I acted as Michael's guide/communicator on most occasions. He played a major part in the campaign for a Scottish equivalent to Section 7 Guidance in England and Wales, taking part in the march along the Royal Mile to the Scottish Parliament in 2005. There he met Margaret Mitchell, MSP, with whom both he and I, and others, had worked closely to get Section 7 on the agenda.

Michael was a founding director of Deafblind Scotland when it became a separate Scottish charity on 31 March 2001. These were both exciting and challenging times causing the occasional sleepless night for most of the deafblind people on the board of directors, not to mention the sighted-hearing directors. He served as vice-chairman to Bob Nolan from 2007 to 2016 when he retired. Throughout his service on the board he made sure that recommendations made at SAGOD meetings were reported at board meetings, and actions to be taken reported back at SAGOD meetings. He asked relevant questions at every meeting I attended with him over the years, always mindful that if he didn't make the point then the point would very likely not be made.

One part of Michael's vital contribution to the work of Deafblind Scotland during my time was undoubtedly the part he played in developing and building the new Learning and Development Centre. He served initially on the Accommodation Sub-group leading to the acquisition of the land, and then on the New Building Group which oversaw the design and build phase. It is a strange phrase to use about a fully blind man, but

Michael always had a keen eye for detail, even although he could see nothing. From the moment I met Michael in 1997 he had had no residual vision at all, which is not common; most people have a small amount. In the design and build phase he would labour to access drawings he couldn't see as I tried to explain in words what was in diagrammatic form. We made tactile models out of cardboard, and in the end from plastic, a scale model which he could feel and get an idea of size and proportion from. He and I walked all over the site several times to give him a sense of location, placement, and size.

And at every New Building Group meeting he asked more questions of architects, design team, and surveyors than anyone else. He never deviated from the quest to ensure this building was as deafblind people would want it to be, entirely suitable for their use, and designed to make their lives easier. I made many comments in this vein, but I am sighted-hearing and my comments did not carry anything like the weight that Michael's did. His hard work undoubtedly made a difference to the "Field of Dreams" outcome.

But before all of that he was part of the deafblind members' drive to raise funds to build their dream, firstly by raising funds to buy the land and, once that was achieved, to raise the rest of the funds needed to build (see Chapter 19).

He was a faithful, committed trustee without whose support the dreams and aspirations of deafblind people would have been much less likely to come to reality.

Having resigned from the Board of Directors in 2018 he now regularly teaches Braille to other deafblind people in the "Field of Dreams" building, as well as enjoying regular games of scrabble. All of this he does in the building he helped to see built.

Maria Crawford

21: Maria Crawford

Maria was born on 26 September 1967 the third of 4 children. She was born with poor sight in her left eye, but coped well and went to mainstream primary and secondary school. She was conscientious at school and worked hard to pass exams.

Maria loved singing and took part in the annual school shows as part of the choir. Like most teenagers in the 1980s she loved pop music, her favourites being Paul Young, George Michael, and Duran Duran.

When she was in senior school she would help with the lower school trips to Aucherawe House in Fort Augustus. She was the House Captain of Iona House in 6th year and treasured her Captain's badge throughout her life.

Due to family illness Maria was tested for the genetic condition Neurofibromatosis type 2 at the age of 17. Less than a year later she had the first of several operations to remove a cluster of tumours behind the left eye and on the acoustic nerve.

After several months of recovery Maria was determined to get on with life and moved to

Edinburgh to study at Moray House College, where she gained a qualification in Community Education. She found joy in working on projects for North Lanarkshire Council, particularly when she was working with young people in deprived areas.

At the age of 21 Maria was diagnosed with a second acoustic neuroma, this time on the right side. Removal of the tumour would lead to Maria becoming profoundly deaf, and affect her balance. This tumour was monitored for several years while Maria determinedly tried to learn to lip-read and to sign in preparation for entering Deaf society. Learning British Sign Language was very difficult for Maria and she mainly relied on Sign Supported English. Her sight was also becoming more problematic.

In 1994 Maria's tumour on the right side had to be removed. Maria became deaf overnight and, although she had tried to prepare herself, the reality was traumatic and the recovery was slow. In the end Maria was never able to return to her work in Community Education.

Deafblind Scotland's guide/communicator service was then made available to Maria and, with their communication and guiding support, Maria adapted to a different kind of independent life. She enrolled in a ceramics course from which everyone received a handmade personal gift. The Deaf Club in Glasgow was her other source of social life and she became a keen bingo player, probably because she won lots of prizes. She attended the Deaf Club every Friday for many years, up until a few weeks before she died.

As part of adapting to deafness Maria was partnered with Petal, her treasured Hearing Dog for the Deaf, and from that day, where Maria went, Petal went, even when she wasn't allowed. Petal, like Maria, rarely took instruction, sometimes not alerting Maria at appropriate times. However, Petal became a local hero, appearing in several local newspapers, when she alerted Maria to a fire in her flat. Petal won a brave dog award. Maria was happy to speak to groups about the benefit of having a Hearing Dog for the Deaf and was well received wherever she went.

She was also a very able representative on deafblindness and represented Deafblind Scotland at a number of meetings and consultations, particularly at all North Lanarkshire local meetings, which she attended on a regular basis. She was never afraid to put a point about the needs of deafblind people and ensured she was kept up to date both in terms of regular information and in terms of the communication support she received at meetings. Petal needed water, and her guide/communicator needed a break, and she let neither down.

She also spoke about Neurofibromatosis when requested and offered support to others in Scotland who suffered from the condition. She often went to the hospice nearby with Petal, where she would be treated to a tasty lunch. She also attended mass there every Sunday.

In 2001 Maria became one of the first directors appointed to the new Deafblind Scotland Board and served the membership well until 2006 when she stepped down due to her health problems for a year, only to be re-elected as soon as her health improved.

She was very familiar with the local hospitals Hairmyres, Gartnavel, Monklands, and the Neurology department at the Southern General Hospital. And her guide/communicators were also familiar with the operating theatres in a few of them as they accompanied Maria during procedures.

She played a large part in discussions about new accommodation, whether it should be rented or bought, in the centre of Glasgow or on the outskirts, and what the risks were. She was committed to Deafblind Scotland's wellbeing and fought her corner throughout the journey to new accommodation always advising caution, and not taking financial risks for new accommodation, especially if it put the organisation and its services at risk.

By the time the building decisions were made her vision was in a poor state. She had had an operation to remove one eye, and replace it with a prosthetic one. And later she had had another operation to help the other eye close more easily, none of which really helped her see more clearly. She regularly had to have eye drops in and gel put in and taking part in meetings was exhausting for her. She was beginning to develop a shake in her head which was making life more difficult for her therefore she stepped down from the board. But her influence had been invaluable.

Maria's main commitment was to her family. She loved her nieces and nephews, Amy, Lara, and Luke. Her favourite time of year was Christmas. She referred to the children as her pride and joy and always made time to play with them. At Christmas the guide would carry in a sack of toys for them and communicate to

Maria the expressions on their faces as they opened them.

Her head shake started to exacerbate her difficulties and made communicating more difficult, eating more difficult, and balance more difficult.

In 2013 Maria's health deteriorated further when she was diagnosed with tumours throughout her body. She showed great strength, determination, and courage in her final years. Her eyesight became very poor and the effort to take in any information was just too great. She could no longer see TV or her Kindle. This made life very lonely and frustrating, and she was sometimes terrified of losing the tiny bit of vision she had left. Anxiety became a constant companion. A small group of guides had long since become like extended family to her, and together with carers from Cornerstone they worked together to help her get as much as she could out of life. She died in hospital on 15 April 2019, aged 41. Guide/communicators described Maria as a fiercely independent woman who was witty, kind, astute, with a wicked sense of humour, who had people down to a tee within minutes.

Chapter 3

Everyday Deafblind Heroes

Deafblind people who meet the definition of deafblindness will normally retain a little useful sight or a little useful hearing, or even a little of both. For people with a severe dual sensory loss, life is inevitably confusing, with little certainty in it. It's a life full of guesswork, a life with lots of jigsaw pieces which they have to pick their way through. Each sensory loss as it occurs exacerbates the effects of any other sensory loss, and adds to the difficulties they endure with gaining information, communicating, and getting around safely.

To deafblind individuals making sense of the world is always hard work, and, sometimes, impossible. If they have skilled communication support they may be able to gather some jigsaw pieces, and then put them together using common sense and guesswork. If they do not have that skilled communication support they cannot acquire the jigsaw pieces needed to even begin using guesswork.

This, amazingly, does not stop some of them from pursuing ambitions, making complaints, starting campaigns, but it does make it much more difficult for them to achieve success in any of these actions. While others may settle for a more peaceful life, they work at achieving the ambition, they pick up the complaint form, they carry a banner. Below I have told the story of a few deafblind people who have gone the extra mile, made heroic efforts to achieve something, to fulfil an ambition, right a wrong, or change things for the better. In some cases they simply kept on going. They are my everyday heroes. They won't appear in any other history but they belong in mine as examples of what uniquely disadvantaged people can achieve. And in all fairness, it has to be said, there are many, many more whose stories I could have included.

Everyday Hero - Frank Thomson

22:Frank Thomson

I met Frank Thomson when he was 21 and thinking of moving to London to work as a tutor of British Sign Language. He had been diagnosed as having Usher Syndrome some time before and was determined to live life to the full until Retinitis Pigmentosa began to seriously reduce his sight. Part of that strategy involved the move to London. My involvement with Frankie at that time was to agree that he should not put off the things he wanted to do, but he should go and do them as the opportunity arose.

I heard from him and about him occasionally over the years until, when he turned 40, he came back to Scotland to stay. Deafblind Scotland celebrated their 25th anniversary of setting up in Scotland in 2014 and Frankie spoke at that event and mentioned the advice I had given him all those years before. He had made a great success of his time in London working as a BSL tutor and he hoped to do the same in Edinburgh, although everything was more difficult now due to his rapidly failing sight.

One of the benefits of his time in London was that he had many friends there whom he continued to see regularly, flying down to London to be met at the airport by one of them who would take him to where he was staying for the weekend. This continuity was of major importance to him as he tried to settle in Scotland and find a new direction for his life.

Then, on 21 March 2017, Frankie boarded a low budget airline plane for a trip to London. His friend Katie had booked the flight online in October 2016 stating that he was profoundly deaf with Usher Syndrome. She booked special assistance for him and, on the day, a guide/communicator took him to meet the Special Assistant who took Frankie through check-in, onto the plane, and into his seat.

Minutes after he had taken his seat he felt his arm being tugged and a Special Assistant who could do slow Deafblind Manual tried to explain what was happening. She told Frankie to come with her. He didn't understand why. She said the crew wanted him to leave the plane. and he was left in no doubt that he had to leave. Later it was said that the pilot had refused to let Frankie fly alone. In the meantime, an airline employee had emailed the contact number she had which was for Katie, who is also profoundly deaf. The email read "We have Mr Thomson with us now. He is unable to travel as he requires a companion. We are unable to communicate with him, are you able to contact me or if you have someone who can contact me on your behalf."

Airline staff put Frankie in a taxi and sent him to Katie's house. Meanwhile Katie was on a bus trying to get to the airport to find him. Katie's neighbours took him in. Katie was emailing the airport from her phone, asking where Frankie was. The reply she received said “He is unable to travel as he requires a companion due to the fact he is both blind and deaf so unable to understand and react to safety instructions.”

The incident was, understandably, in the newspapers. Lots of people got involved, local MP Tommy Sheppard; Deafblind Scotland; Frankie’s mum, Olive; and STV news. The Executive Support Team from the airline got involved with all of these people. Indeed, 6 different representatives from the airline were involved, over time, in trying to investigate the issue, mainly with Katie. And they kept asking for a phone number on which they could phone her; deaf awareness was definitely lacking. They did offer a free flight to Frankie and a passenger, which Frankie found insulting, and there was a mention of £250 compensation for this very upsetting experience. It is worth noting that he had flown alone before on various occasions, including with this low budget airline.

After many weeks a meeting was set up in Edinburgh where interested parties could meet face to face, with a BSL interpreter present for Katie and a guide/communicator supporting Frankie, together with Suzanne from Deafblind Scotland, and me in the role of expert witness. After that meeting with the airline the compensation on offer remained at £250 together with a free flight for Frankie and a companion. My request to the airline was that, if they would not allow Frankie to travel alone then he could be allowed free travel for a guide/communicator twice a year, a similar arrangement to that which exists for deafblind people on a daily basis on public transport. After initially appearing very positive for this idea the idea was then firmly and formally rejected.

Another meeting was offered but never materialised and the negative effect this was having on Frankie became obvious. His confidence hit rock bottom, his trips to London were obviously at an end, his relationship with Katie was affected, not helped by the stress this situation had caused to her. And he felt abused by the airline, but powerless against them. I could see he felt this was happening to Katie and him because he was deafblind and Katie was deaf. This could have far-reaching implications for his level of independence which had always been very high.

I did some research on how ordinary people had taken on the might of the airlines and discovered that an organisation called Centre for Effective Dispute Resolution (CEDR) had been set up by all the airlines to deal with smaller claims. The agreement was that any finding by CEDR would be respected by any airline and any compensation up to a maximum of £10,000 agreed by CEDR would be paid by the airline.

Now that I had retired from Deafblind Scotland I had the free time and I advised Frankie to consider taking this avenue as there was no cost to him or me, the process was free, and some degree of compensation could potentially be accessed via this route. Although Frankie had initially thought he should receive apologies, reassurance it would never happen again, and compensation, it was very obvious that this was highly unlikely to happen. But the finding would be on record and the airline would not have escaped unchallenged. So Frankie agreed to pursue the CEDR formal complaint route. The disadvantage was that it all had to be done online.

We agreed to try. An online portal was established in my name as Frankie's representative. A long conversation by phone took place between Frankie and me via a guide/communicator in order to complete the initial form. Amazingly to me, after a couple of long conversations, CEDR seemed to understand that Frankie and I lived 45 miles apart, that we needed to be in the same room to communicate in a tactile manner, and the only alternative was for me to phone Frankie when he had a guide/communicator, and that had to be carefully timed and arranged. These conversations took place several times until CEDR had all the information they needed and the evidence to back that information up.

After several weeks during which the low budget airline was asked to explain their actions, the CEDR case manager contacted me to advise their findings, that they would inform the airline of these and await their response. I was never informed of their response, it never appeared on the portal, but many weeks later CEDR advised they were suggesting compensation and the amount they were going to recommend, asking if this was acceptable to Frankie. It took a week to get an answer to them and this was taken in good grace. The result was sent to the airline and after several weeks they paid the recommended amount.

This issue was never about money to Frankie, it was about his having to accept ejection from a plane with no explanation, his deaf friend being asked several times to "phone" the airline, his requests for a meeting being ignored, having to accept many different people representing the airline over a few weeks. He wanted to feel he was being listened to, and that he could put up a fight for what he saw as his right. And in the end, using the guide/communicator service and a volunteer, he had been able to participate in, and make decisions about, the whole process of taking his case to CEDR, and getting some compensation from the airline. When the decision had been taken and a payment made to him, his whole demeanour changed. He could actually begin to get over what had happened to him, consign it to the past, and get on with his life as a deafblind man living what is never an easy life. He had made a heroic effort and had made his point.

Everyday Hero - Desmond Smith

23:Desmond Smith

Desmond was born in 1944. He was profoundly deaf from birth, and grew up as a deaf person until he began to lose his sight in his teens. He grew up remaining close to his mum and dad, spending a lot of time with his dad, learning good language skills from him, and they shared a keen interest in Meccano from he was 3 years old and this interest has remained with him to this day.

Desmond attended Donaldson's School for the Deaf, at West Coates. When he left school his visual difficulties, together with his deafness, made getting a job more difficult, and he went from job to job. He developed an interest in photography, having spent a short time working in a photographer's.

He stayed with his mother and father until 1961 by which time he had begun to experience problems with his mental health. Eventually he got a job in a laundry where he stayed for 7 years. He moved to Blindcraft in 1977 where a number of deaf people were involved and communication and conversation were easier for him. He settled into a less stressful environment in Blindcraft and enjoyed a good relationship with many other employees. He was able to access guide/communicator hours while employed there and this did a great deal to open up his life. He finally got his own flat in 2000 and learned to cook and look after himself with the help of a regular guide/communicator service. Jackie Knowles played a major role in this service and others contributed.

I remember when a new guide phoned me concerned that Desmond kept asking to go to the library. I asked why he didn't just take him to the library? He was concerned that his Deafblind Manual and BSL skills were perhaps not at a high-enough level. And why would a deafblind man want to go to a library? I suggested again that he try to do what he had been asked. Later he phoned to say Desmond had kept fingerspelling a reference number, which the guide told a librarian about. Desmond was now fingerspelling a phrase, could it be the name of a book? The librarian led them to that reference number and located there was the book, which was about eye conditions. His father had brought him here to find out about eye conditions.

Meccano remained a major hobby of Desmond's from childhood. With the help of his guide/communicators he was able to explore and extend that interest. From screwing nuts and bolts together with his father in the 1950s, with the help of the guide/communicator service he had developed his Meccano skills and, through time, had become a true Meccano buff, creating enough models to fill his flat twice over. These models included a hammer head crane a few feet high with an electric motor which he made in the 1990s, and a big wheel with an electric engine constructed in 2002. He met and made friends with Robert Brown, another deafblind man who had an interest in Meccano and, through Robert, got involved with the larger Meccano community.

Desmond became a member of the Meccano Society of Scotland which opened up a whole new world for him. He was very different from Robert in that he was fully deaf, fully blind, and used Deafblind Manual to communicate. Slowly but surely the guide/communicator and Desmond worked with other members to implement some basic communication with him. Now he works together with other members to find unusual parts, and they are very helpful to him.

Whenever he can Desmond travels, all over the country, to meet others with the same interest, to exhibit at Meccano shows and exhibitions. He relies on a skilled guide/communicator being available on the date of the exhibition.

Recently he began to teach small groups of deafblind people about Meccano and has found a new challenge, firstly in encouraging others to take an interest in model-making with Meccano, and secondly in patiently teaching people with little or no vision or hearing about the possibilities of enjoying Meccano.

Having known Desmond's mother and father, and the way they fought for their son to get opportunities, I like to imagine they now look down on Desmond with a smile on their faces at how he has overcome many difficulties, has achieved meaningful employment, his own life in his own flat, and, in particular his own much-admired Meccano model collection, together with the standing he now enjoys in the world of Meccano UK-wide. He never gave up, he kept on going to reach his goal.

Everyday Hero - Francis Keane

24: Francis Keane with John Dearie 1997

Francis was born in 1941, the youngest of the family, his older siblings being sisters. He was the only deaf child in the family. He lived with his mum and sisters in Oatlands, Glasgow, and often described himself as a Gorbals man. He went to St Vincent's School for the Deaf in Tollcross and was taught by the nuns there. His sign name was a BSL translation of "Frank with the red hair".

Francis is pictured here, on the left, with his great friend, who was also deafblind, John Dearie, at a Christmas meal out in the early 1990s. They used Deafblind Manual to communicate, interspersed with BSL signs.

Francis told me that when he was young he had played football with Jimmy Johnson. I'm not sure if it was in the street, or when he was part of the squad at Celtic Park. I like to think it was the latter. Francis didn't remember ever having good sight, he possibly thought his poor sight was like everyone else's.

He lived his life as a deaf person, used sign language which he learned in the playground at school – although he did have speech – and going to the Deaf Club when he was old enough, to meet other deaf people. He worked in various jobs, as a lumberjack, felling trees, as a refuse collector. He went from one job to another. At one point, totally fed up with not getting work in Glasgow he set off to hitch-hike to Lancaster. It was a long way. But there he found work as a cook, and that was the start of a new direction work-wise for him, working in kitchens, preparing food. He moved around England doing that for several years. Then his sight loss grew too great making it difficult for him to work, so he returned to Glasgow, and another phase of his life began.

Francis's quality of life had been far from ideal until that point but going forward without sight, without a job, without a partner, without a purpose meant that Francis was far more vulnerable than he had previously been. He no longer felt part of the Deaf community, simply because they use a visual, gestural language, and he could no longer easily catch what they were signing. He might have taken a decision to use, or at least try, a tactile version of sign language, but he didn't and therefore slowly but surely became increasingly cut off.

He began to become more and more anxious about things, about the future, about his sight, about lack of family contact, about letters he received and couldn't read, about money, about health problems. He lived in a constant state of heightened anxiety. And for him, living in that state, he would sometimes be overwhelmed by it, and would resort to alcohol to calm him down and occasionally he could not see a future for himself. He would be taken into hospital, often an incredibly difficult situation for a deafblind person. And after a few days or a week he would be sent home again. In between these episodes he was a very pleasant man, kind and thoughtful and always thinking of others, and almost always anxious.

I met Francis in 1990 soon after Barrowfield Deaf-blind Complex opened. When he moved into his own flat within the complex he and Dorrie Moore became very friendly. Dorrie used only Deafblind Manual, and this encouraged Francis to use Deafblind Manual as well. Sometimes he helped Dorrie to teach Deafblind Manual to people. Deafblind people lived at Barrowfield and also gathered there socially sometimes. Francis got to know deafblind people for the first time in his life.

Deafblind Scotland's new guide/communicator service came into being in 1995 and Francis was one of the first people to benefit from it. The guides were new, he was a new service-user, and they worked with each other to help shape the new service. In the early days Jim and John, 2 new guide/communicators worked with Francis to increase his independence, increase his communication skills, and reduce his anxiety. He loved Elvis and went to the Elvis Club in Glasgow every month, he cycled on a tandem, played dominoes, and learned how to make pottery.

But still there were several hospitalisations over the years. What saved him from serious consequences was the fact that he totally withdrew from everyone when he was in a dark place and could see no future for himself. He would shun interaction with anyone. DBUK staff and guide/communicators were familiar with this and worked to avoid this happening. Finally, after many requests, Dr Paul Davison, a psychiatrist working at the John Denmark Unit, a specialist mental health resource for Deaf people in Manchester, invited Francis to come to Manchester as an inpatient for 3 months and they would work through his issues. He came home calmer and more positive than ever been before and the positive impact lasted for a long time.

However, family was especially important to Francis and he hankered after a life in Telford with his sister and her family. He moved there and stayed there for several years, enjoying it until his sister became ill and could no longer support him in the way he needed. This was a great loss to Francis as, when things had been going well, he had enjoyed living with his sister.

That meant a move back to Glasgow. On his return he moved into Carrgomm, supported accommodation for people with mental health problems. And the guide/communicator service stepped in again in the way it had before, often using the same guides as before. One benefit of living at Carrgomm was that he could have a pet. I'm not sure if it was officially welcomed as a tenant, but a cat moved in with him one day and didn't leave until its death many years later.

Francis's battle with anxiety continued, as did admissions to hospital connected with the anxiety. In between these times he tried manfully to live a normal life. Living that life used a huge amount of energy, governed as it was by his fears. As a deafblind person he was never sure of what was happening, or if he was imagining things, worrying needlessly.

But his kind gentle nature was still to the fore. In the 30 years I knew him he never forgot my birthday, which is in December, close to Christmas. I had once told him birthdays 10 days before and 10 days after Christmas tended to be ignored. We celebrated it every year with an outing which grew over the years. Francis, together with his guide, my husband Hammy, former accountant Allan, and former guide Graham, would all meet for Christmas lunch. Once he told me he missed his old deafblind friend John Dearie and would like to see him sometime. So we included John and his guide each year. It is not easy to arrange a meeting between 2 fully deafblind people who communicate using Deafblind Manual, who can't use a phone or mobile or email, and who both need a guide to get there. But in recent times this was usually the only time they saw each other each year and it was much appreciated by both of them.

We often suggested a nice place for Christmas lunch but Francis's favourite meal was a roll with link sausages, and that's why we went every year to a café at Silverburn which knows how to cook a sausage well. Francis and John would update each other using

Deafblind Manual, and catch up on deafblind gossip. And it was special to all of us to see them happy.

For many deafblind people anxiety is a daily threat. Problems are either caused by, or exacerbated by, not seeing and not hearing. But when Francis could be freed from that anxiety he was easily made happy, easily made to laugh, easily made to enjoy the moment. And his laughter could ring loud in a room. He loved dancing and was the star turn at the Christmas disco. In his younger days he would do a mean impersonation of Elvis singing his favourite "Love me Tender". But when others went home and the door closed behind them the anxiety often took over.

He had had little contact with relatives in recent years so it was lovely to hear that his sister who lived in Glasgow and hadn't seen him for many years had left Francis a legacy in her will, confirming to him that he was important to his family. That was a good year in Francis's life as he was secure in the knowledge that his sister cared about him, and his mental health improved.

My reason for including Francis in the Everyday Heroes section is that he showed a lifetime of courage in fighting his anxieties, and trying to overcome them. This was far from easy for him but he worked at it for all of the 30 years I knew him. He wanted to do the right thing. He kept on going, for his cats, for those around him who mattered to him, for his faith, and because it was the right thing to do. His efforts to do the right thing were heroic and he never gave up on it.

And then in 2019 there was a fire in his house, he was taken to hospital, and he died from smoke inhalation 2 weeks later. During that period all of us who had worked closely with him were by his side, and he knew we were there, and that we considered it a privilege.

Everyday Hero - John Dearie

John was born in Glasgow in 1946. He was profoundly deaf from birth, and like most deaf people sign language was his first language, and deaf culture was where he felt comfortable. And then he began to lose his sight as a young adult. He was diagnosed as having Usher Syndrome. He and his wife Susan, who was also profoundly deaf, had 3 sons and they worked hard to look after them. John worked in George Boyd's Ironmongers, but his job became more difficult as he lost his sight, and he moved to Remploy. He could no longer easily participate in the Deaf community as he once had, or pursue the same interests.

Usher syndrome severely affects peripheral vision but some restricted central vision can remain useful for a long time. And John used this to develop an interest he had had since he was 16 when he had used his good central vision to learn chess via a television programme. Slowly but surely, as he grew more confident, chess became his passion. Through time Rev Stewart Lochrie, from the John Ross Memorial Church in Glasgow, had a special chess board made for John with holes in it which housed the tails on the specially crafted chess pieces. John still uses this board today.

By that time John had no remaining vision, and communicated with others using Deafblind Manual and Hands-on Signing. He could no longer see an interpreter signing, under any circumstances, and struggled to adapt to using tactile communication. In his local area he could happily rely on his guide dog, Ricky, to get him to the local shops etc., but beyond that he needed either a family member or a guide/communicator to safely get around and to communicate with others.

In spite of the fact that chess is a very visual game – not the easiest choice for a blind man – John was always keen to play and had a huge desire to learn. Mike Hooper, Ron Hall, and Ian Frame, local volunteers, have played chess with John every Monday morning since 2000. And this has undoubtedly helped him practise.

25: John Dearie in Germany

John was keen to play in tournaments, especially abroad, but he had 2 major problems in doing that. The first was to identify, and fund, a guide/communicator to go with him. The second problem is that competitive games are time-limited, and it is very time-consuming for John to check where pieces are every time a move is made. However, several associations will allow extra time for deafblind people and John focussed on these tournaments.

During a competition John will play on his own board and his opponent will play on the competition board. The opponent will sit opposite the guide/communicator. When John makes a move, the guide will replicate the move on the competition board. When the opponent makes his move, the guide will take John's hand and copy the opponent's move onto John's own board. The guide will record the moves wherever possible, for information afterwards.

Over the years John also took part in a few deafblind chess competitions, by invitation, and he loved being part of them, as he played on a fully equal basis.

Then Ian Carmichael, from the Scottish Chess and Draughts Association for the Deaf (SCDAD) invited John to be part of the Deaf team attending the World Deaf Chess Championships in Malente, Germany in July 2004. Mike Hooper instantly agreed to accompany him, together with a guide/communicator. John was presented by the mayor with a crystal trophy for "Excellent Sportsmanship" as the first deafblind person to play in the championships. In 2008 John again played as part of the SCDAD group in the St Gallen, Switzerland, World Championships, and in 2010 he played in the World Championship in Estoril, Portugal. Over the years John played as an individual in the deafblind section of some World Championships.

John also played as part of a Deafblind Scotland team in SCDAD national tournaments with deafblind teammates Clark Steven, Robert Dillon, and Gerry Dillon, always achieving good results. John played in sighted-hearing chess clubs in Glasgow. He played as an individual in Scottish Deaf tournaments in Aberdeen, Dundee, Prestwick, Edinburgh, Glasgow, and Fife and has his name on the trophy on more than one occasion. He also took part in tournaments in Sheffield, Liverpool, and Dublin where SCDAD had been invited to take part, and in Chess Scotland's tournaments in Ayr and Dundee. He normally went with one of a small specialist group of guide/communicators who were well schooled in interpreting at a chess tournament. John played in any tournament he could secure support to attend. The pleasure he gains from playing chess is the one thing which brings light to his life.

None of this has been easy for John to achieve. Often tournaments last for a week and there are games all day. John uses only Tactile BSL and Deafblind Manual to communicate, which means only highly skilled people can support him. There is no doubt he should have 2 guide/communicators over a week-long tournament. But the costs would be substantial, and funding for this is not easily available, the result of which is that he has rarely attended a national or international tournament in recent years.

Clear in my memory is a picture of John at around 40 with the first of his 4 guide dogs, Ricky, (later he had Warren, then Innes, and then Umber). A fully deafblind man and his dog, a tight little unit, involving a dog which understood enough signs to obey and support his owner on his home turf. This little unit, however, would struggle to get safely to any unknown destination, even local ones. But the deafblind chess-playing owner could, amazingly, take part in national and international chess tournaments. He has trophies to prove it. The strength of character needed to do this is incredible. He is an everyday hero in overcoming all the barriers facing a deafblind chess player.

Everyday Hero - Clark Steven

26: Clark Steven

Clark was born in 1960 in East Kilbride to Tommy and Susan. He was profoundly deaf from birth, as was his sister, while his brother was born hearing.

Clark attended the Deaf School in Hamilton where, at that time, signing was not encouraged and children were instead encouraged to learn speech. He remembers that they all signed to each other in the playground and gained sign language skills in this way. The family spent each summer on a farm in Killygordon in Ireland, where Clark remembers playing all day long with friends Michael, Gerry, and Sammy. Communication wasn't a problem. It rarely is a problem when young, and particularly during play. He enjoyed going to BB on a Friday night where one of the officers, Alex Calder, took an interest in ensuring he got his badges and also that he enjoyed the process of getting them.

As a boy his grandfather took him to watch Celtic play on a Saturday and there his lifelong love of football began. He had good sight at that time and, unlike many other activities for profoundly deaf people, football was ideal. With its colour, movement, excitement, and clear objectives football was something he could be fully involved in, that is, until he began to lose his sight.

As was common at that time, Clark's mum and dad had been advised early on not to encourage their deaf children to use sign language in order to promote development of speech. And they followed that advice. Fingerspelling and familial signs were used by the family and Clark and Anne signed to each other all the time. However, communication between parent and child was often less than comprehensive and misunderstandings were common.

For Clark and Anne, however, their need to develop a range of communication methods would become more urgent as they were both diagnosed as having Usher Syndrome, a condition which causes deafness from birth and sight loss due to Retinitis Pigmentosa starting in the teens. This meant sight loss at some point was inevitable and Clark was aware of his sight loss at age 12.

At that time there were few options for a young deaf person with sight loss and securing a job was then, and remained, the height of his ambitions. He started work in Blindcraft at 16, and spent some time in Blindcraft in Torquay, and in Letchworth Engineering Company. However, this path did not lead to a satisfying working life.

When I met Clark in the early 1990s he was almost fully blind, used sign language to communicate to me, and barely understood what I was saying when I used Deafblind Manual to communicate with him. The spelling was obviously a problem as is often the case with deafblind people who are fluent sign language users, but for whom English spelling has not been high on their agenda at school.

He was going through a difficult period, having moved back with his parents after his marriage had ended. He was suffering from anxiety, was unable to see any future for himself, and didn't have a job, so his life had lost its shape. He was incredibly cut off from the world, in every way. Almost inevitably he had become depressed.

His mum and dad were growing older and were less able to offer all of the support he needed, and in particular he needed specialised communication support. This was frustrating for all of them. It was agreed that Clark should move into his own accommodation. My role was to help him secure accommodation and to ensure that, when he moved into new accommodation, he got the guide/communicator service he needed.

Apart from all the everyday difficulties, my ambition was to address the lack of any joy in his life. He was a young man and needed interests, his own home, a reason to go out sometimes. And just as importantly, the means to go out, and the necessary communication support to accomplish tasks while he was out.

I spoke to the council, arranged a meeting with Social Work for Clark, and as soon as they were aware of the need they agreed to work to meet it. This involved developing a small group of highly skilled guide/communicators who would have BSL skills close to BSL interpreter level. And at that time there were few interpreters around, far less skilled guide/communicators. In Deafblind Scotland we had set out some time before to develop a small group of specialist professionals to address the need in Scotland, particularly in the Central Belt.

Clark was happy to move to a house of his own which was adapted for his needs. He was close to Mum and Dad and they could continue to give support as he established himself in his new home. And now was the time for Clark to open up his life. After many discussions about what he might do there were 3 objectives he wanted to achieve in his life – getting a job, learning new skills, and finding a partner.

He was interested in aromatherapy, enjoyed a massage, and, in 1996, was persuaded to try a college course in aromatherapy at Glasgow City College. The college were keen for this to be a positive experience for Clark, and also for the tutors involved. So we worked to remove barriers, for example we arranged for Clark to teach other students Deafblind Manual so they could have a basic conversation with him.

Clark could still travel by train if he were dropped off at the station and met at his destination. so that's how we provided a service for the aromatherapy course. His dad, Tommy, took Clark to the station, put him on the train, and a guide/communicator met him off the train in Glasgow Central. Mobiles were not in regular use in 1994/5 when Clark first got a service so it was an act of faith to wait for him to come off a train.

His guide/communicator on some days was Janet Gilroy who was a qualified aromatherapist with great BSL skills, and this helped a lot with devising signs for a vocabulary which was new to Clark. He was allowed to do his assessments using sign language and Deafblind Manual. He completed the course and gained the certificate he had aimed for. This was the start of a more open life for Clark.

In 1998 he obtained a work experience placement in a factory making and fixing wheelchairs. He was a natural. He was granted a guide/communicator service for a few hours each day to accompany him to and from the factory and to go over any instructions he needed. He liked working there and would have been happy to stay. But it was not considered a viable option for either Clark or the company. Apparently to qualify for a sponsored placement the individual had to be able to produce 80% of normal output and this was not achievable. Getting a worthwhile job was difficult.

I thought it would be good if he tried going back to a football match, but he wouldn't hear of it; his signed answer was "what's the point when I can't see the game?" He also thought people might stare. I asked him what he missed most from his past life as a sighted deaf person, and without hesitation he said he missed going to a football match. I told him we could make it happen if he would just try it.

At that time I ran a youth football team, so I understood what was involved in watching a football match. And I began to think about what would be involved in interpreting one into Deafblind Manual. I had recently gained a Deafblind Manual (DBM) Interpreter qualification and felt interpreting a football match was quite possible, particularly if the DBM interpreter knew about football. Clark had focussed on improving his spelling and on his English comprehension in the time we had known each other, so, between us, we were in a good position to try to make this happen for Clark. But despite my reassurances he didn't see how he would get enough out of the experience.

Then along came the World Cup in 1998 and his interest in football was re-awakened by the prospect of Scotland playing Brazil in France on 10 June at 4.00pm. So we watched that game on TV; if I remember correctly, I think in the pub; and I interpreted it to him. He got the idea. For the first time he was interested.

It was a stroke of luck that 2 new guide/communicators came on board at that time, Christine and Margaret-Anne, within weeks of each other. They were both fluent BSL users and, after undergoing guide/communicator training, worked to become fast Deafblind Manual users. Both Christine and Margaret-Anne were naturally enthusiastic people and this worked well for Clark, encouraging him to get involved in being a football fan again.

Margaret-Anne was a huge Celtic fan so when she was the guide/communicator she was happy to interpret a Celtic match from TV. I wanted to try interpreting a live game and Celtic Football Club cooperated with us in doing this. We had 3 free seats in the disabled or wheelchair section and we went to a game to see how it might work. While there were benefits from being at a live game there were also disadvantages. The disabled seats are right beside the park, on the same level. While you are close to the action the guide/communicator actually gets a poor view of the rest of the park, so the information absorbed and then conveyed is limited.

27: Clark Steven and C. Lawler being recorded for Celtic TV

People did look, but only because they were fascinated by the communication happening in front of them. Clark was hooked, and he was also exhilarated by the experience. But we guides were using only Deafblind Manual and at great speed, which was exhausting for both parties. It was a paraphrased version of the game he received in these days. We developed a few new tactile football signs to reduce the time-lag between the action happening and the information getting across.

When the first goal was scored, Clark immediately knew about it; it was a physical experience. Thousands of people stood up in a split second and jumped around. He couldn't stop smiling. I held his hands up in the air and shook them in celebration when the goal was scored. But he knew before I did that.

As time went on his support team, Margaret-Anne, Christine, and I worked together to develop skills in how we might interpret a football match, with much of it coming from Clark himself. The idea emerged to use Clark's left hand as the pitch; it was a game-changer, a stroke of genius in terms of communication. The tips of the fingers and the heel of the hand were the goals and the centre line was at the top of the palm. The forefinger traces the movement of the ball on the palm. All the while the players' names involved in any action are fingerspelled on the palm. The secret lies in the direction of play being clearly conveyed. And when the ball went out of play the forefinger traced the direction it took.

He bought a season ticket for a seat with a good view, which, apart from making it easier for his guide, gave him access to a lounge. There he met lots of other fans who quickly learned to communicate with him. When I took him to a game a few months later I was amazed to see how many people came up to communicate in Deafblind Manual with him. Just sharing basic communication may not seem a lot, but it was wonderful for a young deafblind man to have people greet him in his own language. This was the advantage of having 2 enthusiastic guides working with him at Celtic Park. They worked to integrate him into the fan group, which has now become a group of "Bhoys" who are friends for life. They keep in touch by email, which the guides interpret for him in Tactile BSL, they enjoy an annual outing to Ayr races, and they were guests when Clark married Eliza in 2016. A lovely day when Christine was Clark's guide/communicator and Rosaleen was Eliza's. Eliza is also deafblind but has some speech. She and Clark had been friends for years before their relationship developed further. They obviously have no communication problems as both are fluent Hands-on-Signing users as well as Deafblind Manual users.

Highlights of his life as a fan include trips to away games in every ground in Scotland; a trip with Margaret-Anne to Annfield Stadium to watch Celtic v Liverpool, and with Christine when she accompanied him to Seville to watch Celtic v Porto in the UEFA Cup

Final. (You can read how Margaret-Anne got him tickets for the game in Chapter 12.)

It would have been easy for Clark to stay at home, isolated and alone, believing that football was no longer for him, and thus avoiding the risk of disappointment when he failed to connect with it again. But in the end he took a chance, made a heroic effort to find ways to make it work for him, ways which could be sustained. And he succeeded. He became a football fan again. And that took great courage and dedication. He became one of only a handful of fully deafblind football fans in UK who regularly attend games

Everyday Hero - Carol Fulton

Carol was born in the 1960s, to a large family. She had real hearing problems from birth, and was the second deaf child in the family. She was sent to a School for the Deaf, joining her sibling who was already there as a boarder. Monday to Friday they signed in the playground at school. At the weekend they struggled with communication with family.

Through time it was noticed that they both had a sight problem as well, which eventually would be diagnosed as the Retinitis Pigmentosa associated with Usher Syndrome. The family had barely come to terms with their deafness and this sight problem was a devastating blow. The siblings meanwhile were unaware other people didn't see the same way they did, so they just tried to get on with life.

Carol left school without qualifications, ill prepared for work in the hearing world. She got a job, then another, and was desperately unhappy. The only relief was the Deaf Club when she could meet with deaf people and communicate in sign language. Then a hearing man at work took an interest in her, too much of an interest as it turned out, and she became pregnant. The relationship ended very quickly.

When the baby was born she left hospital with a social worker who did what she could for the young mother, arranging basics for the baby, and then Carol was left pretty much alone to try to look after both of them. She didn't know what to do, she needed communication support, as well as support with the baby and that wasn't possible. She inevitably became depressed.

Her family tried to help, but her mother sadly died when Carol's daughter was young. She eventually got some part-time work when someone could help look after her baby and worked variously as a cleaner, in Remploy, in a factory, anywhere really where the hours suited. By now her sight loss was getting worse and affecting her ability to get, and hold down a job, at the ripe old age of 30.

Then she met a deaf man, and got married. He could sign, and life was good, then her daughter played truant from school. I got involved as part of my role at Deafblind Scotland and was immediately impressed by her care for her daughter. I succeeded in improving her benefits and I tried to help with her daughter and schooling. But the regular support needed for Carol just wasn't there. At that time Carol had only just started to access a guide/communicator service for 2 hours a week. Not enough to help her cope with a daughter who was struggling.

But worse was to come when her daughter stopped going to school altogether. The social worker referred her to a Children's Panel who decided, over a series of meetings, that Carol could not cope. I attended one meeting and begged the panel to put in the extra support that was needed to help Mum help her daughter, but the decision was that her daughter be sent to a secure unit. She had truanted from school, was 14, and was placed in accommodation within the secure unit with others including a 21-year-old boy who had committed serious crimes. Carol immediately raised her concerns, to no avail. Carol's daughter left that secure unit a year later with all sorts of problems she hadn't had when she went in; she came out a broken person. Which broke Carol too.

But Carol worked at rebuilding their relationship. Her daughter was taking drugs and had a baby so Carol tried to help her in any way she could. They were some distance away, in housing which was unsuitable for her husband who was disabled.

Unable to get an exchange to another council house they eventually took a leap of faith and bought a wee terraced house nearer to the daughter and her child, making it easier to help them both. The financial argument was clear cut. Buying the wee house cost little more than they were paying to rent the flat. It all seemed to make sense. And Carol was determined to try to help her daughter and grandchild, while she still had sight to do so.

Around 2004 she was finally given a guide/communicator service, funded through Supporting People. for just 12 hours a week, but it gave her support to read mail, make phone calls, make appointments, go to the bank, learn things, occasionally go to the Deaf Club to communicate in sign language. It was a free service, and Carol felt it almost succeeded in replacing the interpreting service she had been able to access when she was Deaf only, with no sight loss. Her relationships and therefore her life improved.

Then her sight began to deteriorate dramatically until she had no remaining useful sight, and was relying on her really poor hearing. She couldn't see her husband signing, and was trying to use Deafblind Manual with him, a man for whom spelling was a real challenge. Certain voices she could hear, but only a few. Hands-on interpreting didn't work for her either. Every day was a struggle. Her daughter tried to help Carol now.

Then another scheme was introduced called Self Directed Support. Ken from Deafblind Scotland informed Carol the government intended to give disabled people more choice and control, and he helped Carol fill in a number of forms. She was assessed as needing 12–14 hours of guide/communicator support each week. There would be a financial assessment and she would need to contribute. She didn't understand why an interpreting service was free when she was Deaf only, but now when she was blind she would have to pay for a guide/communicator service. It felt like discrimination to her. But she didn't mind contributing to the service as her contribution was initially estimated as being £26 per week.

Then the real bombshell came when, some time later, they calculated what her contribution would be. Every penny which came into the house was treated as income including both her husband's and her disability allowances. Then all the household expenses were added up – except, crucially, the £400 per month paid out for the mortgage. That was not allowable as a household expense. When calculations were complete she was told her contribution would be approximately £165 per week.

She could not possibly afford to pay that amount and to live anything like a normal life. Being deafblind is an expensive way of life; you have to use taxis to get places, you need to pay for 2 to get into anything, you can't use the internet to get bargains, you tend to buy ready meals which are easier than trying to cook, and you need special equipment often not available free. So Carol had to refuse the service as it required a contribution of £165 per week.

That was in 2014, the last time she had a Social Work assessment. Since then she has existed on 3 hours of service per week from Deafblind Scotland which she pays for herself, 3 hours to do what she used to take 12 to do. Obviously it didn't work. No more trips to the Deaf Club, no more meetings with other deafblind people. No more learning.

Now communicating had become almost impossible. She tried to use the same 2 guides who have a voice at a certain tone, which she can hear better than others. If she had an important meeting she wanted to wait until she could have one of those guides, or myself, and Katy from the Advocacy Project. We had been involved with her for a long time, and she could hear enough of what we said if we sat close to her.

There had been a long history between Social Work and Carol and it had not always been a positive experience for her. But she soldiered on trying to get the support she needed – a guide/communicator service for which she was prepared to pay a lot less than what was being asked of her. She used her advocate to help her make a complaint to the Social Work service, and then to take it to the next level, and then to take it to the Ombudsman.

Her life during that period became focussed on trying to remember incidents, looking for documents, evidence, to prove she had been unfairly treated. When you have a uniquely disabling condition such as deafblindness it is a very negative experience to focus on proving to people that you need a lot of help, you need special arrangements to be made for you. I acted as guide/communicator at several meetings. It took a heroic effort for a deafblind person to try to prove that she was at a huge disadvantage, and to people she believed should know the disadvantage she suffered.

Sadly, the Ombudsman could not look at the council charging policy which did not allow mortgage payments as a household expense. This was for the simple reason that it was time-expired, i.e. it was more than a year since the assessment decision had been made.

Social Work had said Carol was uncooperative about coming to meetings, insisting on having her own communicators attend. So although Carol did not win any major victory re the mortgage payment issue, the Ombudsman did recommend that she should have 4 weeks' notice of any meeting to take place with Social

Work so that she could properly prepare in terms of communication support and access to documents. And that, for her, has made a tremendous difference because she could arrange her own communication support and choose those she best understood.

In 2019 she had an assessment, the first in which she felt she had fully participated. At the time of writing she is hoping to start receiving a basic service at a cost she can afford, mainly due to reaching an age where she qualifies for a 50% discount. The outcome which matters most to her is that she will now get 4 weeks' notice of any Social Work meeting, courtesy of that recommendation made by the Ombudsman. This recommendation has created a new situation and enabled a relationship between Carol and a helpful social worker to finally develop along positive lines.

Some time ago Carol said to me

> "I have to believe Social Work simply don't understand how much I need a guide/communicator, how much support I need to be able to take part in a meeting, how much time to prepare, and to follow up. I need them to understand.
>
> I feel I am being punished for becoming deafblind, and also for having a mortgage. If I were in a rented property my rent would qualify as expenditure – my mortgage doesn't – if it did I would have a guide/communicator service at a reasonable cost. If I were only Deaf I would have a BSL interpreter for free. So I feel I am being punished for becoming blind.

> Drena said I am one of the Everyday Heroes, a deafblind person who comes up against barriers all the time, often the same barriers, and I keep trying to get these barriers removed. I don't think that makes me a hero."

I think it does make Carol, and other deafblind people like her, heroes, all of them. It takes energy, commitment and tenacity to keep trying to take barriers down. Everyday life is so difficult for deafblind people, and most just cannot make the effort needed to keep going. Carol Fulton kept going.

Everyday Hero - John Smith

28: John Smith

John was born deaf and had cataracts in both eyes. Over the years attempts were made many times to remove them, until he was 18, when it became pointless. John could hear noise, but could not discern what was being said. Friends made a fool of him when he was young, and that may be the reason he grew up able to stand up for himself.

"It's a hard life and very difficult when you can't communicate," he explained. He would have liked to be the same as the rest of his family, their lives were full with lots to do, and he couldn't join in with most of it. But he enjoyed Boy Scouts, and then Boys Brigade, and church activities as they made an effort to include him.

As a Deaf child in a hearing family life was not always easy. His brother was 2 years older than John and liked to frighten him during the night when he was coming back from the toilet. John would scream with fright when he saw him. So John's father belted both of them, his brother for scaring John, and John for screaming in the middle of the night.

He discovered a love of football while he was at school and he played for Govan Amateurs when he was 20, in the same team as Alex Ferguson who later became manager of Manchester United. He got a few red cards. His father and brother used to come see him play and he enjoyed that very much. John couldn't hear the referee's whistle so the ref waved a hankie as well. He could see enough to see the ball – sometimes – at that point. John felt football was one place where no one was bothered if he was deaf with poor sight, he was a good player, so he was accepted.

Having started his working life in a milk factory he moved to a job in a bakery when he was 17. When he could no longer read the recipes, he went back to the hospital where they operated on one eye telling him at the time that he would become completely blind when he got older.

He married Margaret, who was also profoundly deaf and a sign language user, when he was just 21. They met on a joint outing of all the Glasgow Deaf Clubs to Dunoon, on the Waverley paddle steamer. As John and Margaret had a family and they grew up he wanted them to be treated fairly and didn't like it if he felt they were disadvantaged by having deaf parents.

When he had problems he contacted those with responsibility for that area of service. This included the council, Social Work department, and roads department. He was not easily dissuaded and often stuck with his quest for justice well beyond what others would do.

In a similar way he felt that deafblind people got a raw deal and he didn't like it. He became a member of Deafblind Scotland in the 1990s and immediately saw that deafblind people weren't fighting for their rights, for better services.

He was always willing to help them in any way he could. The Scottish Advisory Group on Deafblindness was a forum for deafblind people to air their views and John was never reticent about putting someone right in that setting. As chief executive of Deafblind Scotland, that "someone" was occasionally me. SAGOD attracted able people and together they made a formidable group who knew, for example, how to get answers from a visiting politician. I viewed their honesty, forthright manner, and persistence as an encouragement to other deafblind people to have the courage to make their point. And I was often pleasantly surprised by the number of visiting professionals and politicians who appreciated their candour, and willingness to speak.

In 2001 Section 7 Guidance was introduced in England and Wales by the UK government. This gave deafblind people in England and Wales rights they had not previously enjoyed, including the right to an assessment by a specialist worker, and the right to a guide/communicator service, amongst others. It was a great moment and most of us were of the opinion it was just a matter of time before the Scottish government would introduce similar guidance. Particularly if we lobbied the Scottish Parliament...

29: March with Anne Dobbie. Margaret Mitchell MSP, M. Tervitt, Michael Anderson and David McLetchie MSP, 2005

John and Michael Anderson, amongst others, were committed to getting this guidance replicated in Scotland. John visited his local MSP, Margaret Mitchell, and the campaign to get Section 7 Guidance replicated in Scotland began. Margaret had been helpful to John with smaller issues and she had taken a great interest in, and been helpful to Deafblind Scotland over the years, but this campaign meant persuading the Scottish parliament to take a new direction. However, John was persuasive and in March 2005 Margaret put forward a motion in the Scottish Parliament seeking for Scotland the equivalent to Section 7 Guidance in England and Wales, which read:

30: On our way to the Scottish Parliament, 2005

> "Deafblindness – That the parliament recognises the European Parliament Declaration of Rights of Deafblind people which was formally adopted on 1st April 2004 and recognises deafblindness as a distinct disability separate from hearing or sight

> impairment; considers that more should be done to identify, correctly assess and provide appropriate services for this unique group who cannot automatically benefit from mainstream services or services for people who are either blind or deaf, and further considers that councils should make appropriate provision for this uniquely disadvantaged group, ensuring that they have the same provision of services as outlined in the guidance issued under section 7 (1) of the Local Authority Social Services Act 1970 for England and Wales."

On 9 March 2005 a group of 40 deafblind people accompanied by their guide/communicators left from Lenzie Station, with banners saying "Is there life after deafblindness?", "We can't see, we can't hear, will you listen?", "Equality for deafblind Scots", and "Why can't Deafblind Scots have Section 7 Guidance?" They took the train to Edinburgh to join others coming from the length and breadth of Scotland. After a quick lunch they lined up and started to march down the High Street to the Scottish Parliament waving banners and blowing whistles. Members from Inverness and the Scottish Borders joined them at the Scottish Parliament around 4.00pm creating a group some 100 strong. Most were dressed in their red and white Deafblind Scotland T-shirts. There was a Scotland v Wales rugby match on that day, and with Welsh fans being dressed in red and white, there was a sea of red and white in Edinburgh's Royal Mile.

Having arrived at parliament, more than 20 MSPs were waiting to meet their constituents, and Cathie

Craigie and Margaret Mitchell joined the group. The deafblind people took their place in the gallery before the debate started. They made quite a sight with all the forms of communication being used by guide/communicators and BSL interpreters to interpret the debate for the deafblind people. Twelve MSPs spoke in support of the motion, with 64 MSPs putting their name to it, which was more than we had hoped for. There was a small reception afterwards where Rhona Brankin and others had a further chance to meet deafblind people, guide/communicators, and staff. It was a great day, and John was delighted. Margaret, his MSP, had proposed the motion to get an equivalent to Section 7 Guidance implemented in Scotland.

For all the things deafblind people had got involved in as individuals or in small groups, nothing compared to that day. They were out in front with banners, making demands of the Scottish Parliament, their individual MSPs, and ministers. They weren't supporting another organisation. This was their particular fight and they were leading the charge. And they did it magnificently. And then they went home and waited.

However, when time passed, it became apparent that an equivalent to Section 7 Guidance was not going to materialise for Scotland. The parliament had decided to find its own way for deafblind people and that was as part of a plan for all 3 sensory impairments.

This was the chosen route for the Scottish Parliament, and it was destined to disappoint deafblind people. John knew that, as did I, and our disappointment was palpable. But he never stopped putting the case, he knew it would improve the lives of deafblind people.

John has never, ever given up fighting for the rights of deafblind people, and he has met with some success. He may have ruffled a few feathers sometimes, but he has also inspired others to believe that they can make a difference, and bring about change. And in doing that, he, and others, have truly been leaders.

Having suffered a stroke, John's ability to get involved with campaigns became more limited. His wife Margaret also began to suffer health problems. And when her poor health meant she needed more help he put her needs first, ensuring her needs were listened to.

However, they have continued to attend SAGOD, and to support fundraising for "Field of Dreams" in every way they could. They never missed a fundraising event. He has never lost his determination that deafblind people should be treated fairly, should have the same rights as deaf people, and the same rights as others across the UK. It takes courage, tenacity and a dose of heroism to mount such a campaign, and it takes even more heroism to accept a negative result and keep going, seeking whatever benefits can be gained for deafblind people. And John just keeps on going.

Conclusion

There are many other Everyday Deafblind Heroes who went above and beyond their own expectations, including: Agnes Fisher who wrote and published a book about her life as a deaf person; Evelyn Brown who wrote a book about inspirational people, all of whom were blind or deafblind; Chris Nicol, a young deafblind man who fought against great odds to take part in the 2019 Karate World Championships in Slovakia; James Peline who had been a boxer in his youth and plucked up the courage to go back to boxing training in his sixties; and Robert Dillon who taught himself to play chess with help from volunteers at Deafblind Scotland and played for several years in hearing chess clubs which were closer to home. He went on to win not only a Deafblind Scotland competition but a Deaf Club competition too. If tactile sign language is your normal way of communicating, any of the achievements listed here take a heroic effort to achieve, as well as the support of a skilled guide/communicator. And mention should be made of all the deafblind directors, particularly those who signed up to take on the responsibility of being directors of a brand-new charity in 2001. They are listed in Chapter 13. These are just a few examples of deafblind people stepping forward. There are others, too numerous to mention. It took courage to do all of these things, something most deafblind people have in abundance, and use every day, just to get on with normal life.

Chapter 4

Deafblindness

Somewhere, in a book about deafblindness, it seems wise to assume that some readers will have little knowledge of this condition. Indeed, another whole book could and should be written about the condition of acquired deafblindness. In this chapter we will look at a definition of deafblindness which has been in use for many years, the potential numbers, one main cause of deafblindness, and some of the implications of having this uniquely disabling condition.

In the United Kingdom the following description of deafblindness was first introduced in the report "Breaking Through: developing services for Deafblind People" (1988, Deafblind Services Liaison Group, p.6):

> "Persons are regarded as deafblind if they have a severe degree of combined visual and auditory impairment resulting in problems of communication, information and mobility."
>
> (The Department of Health Guidance)
>
> "Care and Support for Deafblind Children and Adults" issued in 2014 continues to use the broad definition:
>
> Persons are regarded as deafblind if their combined sight and hearing impairment cause difficulties with communication, access to information, and mobility."
>
> (Sense UK)

This description includes both congenital and acquired deafblindness. This chapter is focussed on those who have acquired deafblindness, usually as an adult, although some of the points may also be pertinent to those who have congenital deafblindness.

I very much viewed as a strength the use of the words “are regarded” when I began to use this definition, as it inferred that this is how we might describe this person’s condition, perhaps from the perspective of needs, statistics, or providing services. Deafblind may well not be the word an individual would use to describe themselves. Indeed, they might be very reluctant to use that description.

During the work to develop the Scottish Executive Data Standards for Dual Sensory Impairment it was found that individuals did not describe their condition in a single word, but were more likely to describe their “route” to dual sensory impairment using terms such as: Deaf with a visual problem; Blind with a hearing loss; Hearing and sight impaired; Deaf with Usher Syndrome; Partially sighted and partially hearing; Profoundly Deaf and partially sighted. In a 25-year career less than a handful of people described themselves to me as Deafblind on our first meeting. This includes even those who use Deafblind Manual or Hands-on Signing to communicate.

Reliable data collection on deafblindness has historically been problematic with estimated numbers varying from 11,000 in the UK provided in the Breaking Through report of 1988, to 21,000 in the UK in 1996 from RNIB. The same number was given by Deafblind Services Liaison Group (DBSLG; who published the Breaking Through report, 1988) in July

1997, i.e. 21,000 in the UK or an incidence of 40:100,000. In 2004 the European Parliament Written Declaration Article 13 which recognised "deafblindness as a distinct disability" quoted "there are about 150,000 people in the European Union who are deafblind". Current UK estimates of dual sensory impairment are around 365,000 with the preponderance being older people who have suffered sensory loss in later adulthood. My experience with Deafblind Scotland led me to believe that 10% of those who had a dual sensory loss were fully deafblind, and mainly reliant on tactile communication.

The See Hear Strategic Framework suggested the number of people in Scotland who might identify themselves as fitting within the "Breaking Through" definition would probably be around 5000, i.e. those who have a severe loss of both sight and hearing, creating sustained ongoing daily difficulties with communication, access to information, and getting around.

At this level deafblindness would be considered a low-incidence disability, and the consequence of that is that the general public are unfamiliar with the condition or the problems it brings. They may know someone who has a sight and hearing impairment and this causes them to struggle, they will not have met a tactile communication user. This requires deafblind people to give explanations about their needs on a daily basis, which is disabling at best.

Where a little residual sight and/or hearing remains, the deafblind condition can often be misunderstood, occasionally even challenged. The number of people in that category can only be estimated as they will often be hidden within the Deaf community or the Blind community. And the level of difficulty experienced is often underestimated. The level of lighting available, background noise, the tone of the voice can seriously affect communicative interactions in unexpected ways. Deafblindness is a disability which inflicts a unique type of isolation on those who suffer from it; caused by communication breakdown; by being physically unable to safely travel alone; by being deprived of information, with potentially devastating effects longer term. Television news items, newspapers, the internet are inaccessible to many of them and therefore information which other people may have is totally new to them.

Deafblind people access information often via alternative formats including Braille, Moon, large print, extra-large print, audio, BSL DVDs, and tactile sign language – usually provided by a guide/communicator. The effort required to obtain information can simply become too great. For many deafblind people the use of tactile communication methods is such hard work, it can become an unacceptable price to pay to access information, so they simply give up. Trying to learn a tactile communication method once sight and hearing have seriously deteriorated is very difficult.

I have also witnessed the arrival of a tome of brailled information for a deafblind person who can read grade 1 Braille as used in a simple letter. Merely transposing a long document into Braille is rarely enough to give genuine access. Brailling an Executive Summary of a document with more information being made available if required may be a more helpful way to do it, and the person has enough basic information to get started.

Governments have historically appeared to believe that measures put in place to help the visually impaired and the hearing impaired will automatically benefit those who are deafblind. This is understandable in some ways, but it is a dangerous misconception. While those who have a dual sensory loss will benefit from some measures put in place for a single sensory impairment this cannot automatically be assumed to work for all. Deafblind people simply don't have the "compensating sense" that those who have a single loss still retain. Deaf people rely on vision, blind people rely on hearing, to "compensate".

They need specialist services focussed on communication support, access to information, and specialist guiding. The European Parliament Written Declaration Article 13 of 2004 which recognised "deafblindness as a distinct disability" seems to have been forgotten in recent years, particularly as governments have become involved in major Social Work changes, e.g. to merge Health and Social Care services. All deafblind people require help with communication, access to information, and guiding. However, the type and amount of help needed will vary greatly from person to person, and nothing should be taken for granted. One generalisation I will make is that the deafblind person having speech is a great advantage to those offering help in that it is easier to understand what is needed. But if often misleads the helper into thinking there is little problem with communication, when indeed there is. Having speech does not equal having hearing.

A defining feature of deafblindness as a unique impairment is the notion of synergy: i.e. the sum (deafblindness) is greater than the parts (hearing and vision impairment). It prevents the deafblind person from using one sense to compensate for the loss of the other. It prevents living as what might be described as a poorly functioning single sensory-impaired person. Most importantly, no matter what the degree of deafblindness, it inevitably affects their ability to easily access language, communication, information, and even their physical environment. As Deafblind International have noted, "Two sensory impairments multiply and intensify the impact of each other creating a severe disability which is different and unique."

On behalf of deafblind people, in response to questions about how deafblind people could be involved in public consultations documents, I regularly made the following response: "If you don't make special arrangements to involve deafblind people, they will not be included. They do not automatically access any news item, it requires special arrangements to be put in place to include them." And when arrangements are put in place to provide a guide/communicator service then deafblind people can access the consultation documents, information on meetings, questionnaires, and they can be meaningfully involved and contribute to plans for the future.

Deafblindness is a combined loss of distance senses which robs the person of information gained by those senses. Most of the information we absorb, acquire or assimilate, is from our distance senses. Diminution of these senses leaves us increasingly dependent on touch and smell, which are near senses. By their very nature near senses can only function in a small space therefore severe dual sensory impairment imposes a diminished world, and a reliance on touch.

There are many causes of deafblindness, a whole smorgasbord of eye conditions and ear conditions which can collaborate to create sensory failure over a period of years, sometimes many years, and there are also genetic conditions which cause dual sensory loss from a young age, one of which is worthy of special mention, and which causes sensory difficulties from day one.

Usher Syndrome

Usher Syndrome is a recessive genetic condition which causes hearing loss from birth and gradual visual loss due to Retinitis Pigmentosa often becoming noticeable in the teens and twenties. There are several types of Usher Syndrome, 3 of the most common being:

Type 1 occurs when profound deafness is present from birth, and the individual may grow up using sign language and then experience visual loss in the teens. There can be emotional trauma engendered by the loss of the second sense, or they may assume everyone sees in the way they do. Children may have noticeable balance problems. One real advantage of being a sign language user is that a potential tactile version of BSL could become very helpful when sight diminishes. It is estimated that 3–6% of the born deaf population have the Usher gene, and it has been suggested that Usher Syndrome accounts for 50% of all hereditary deafblindness (see www.nidcd.nih.gov.health-us).

Type 2 Usher Syndrome involves the person being born hard of hearing, with English normally becoming their first language. They have the same visual problem as in Type 1 Usher, i.e. Retinitis Pigmentosa, which causes reduced peripheral vision in the teens or twenties. They are not normally native sign language users and when their sight is reducing tactile sign language or Deafblind Manual are not the most easy options for them to learn, but putting in the effort while they have useful vision is a very sensible step to ensuring effective communication skills, and easy access to language in the future.

Type 3 Usher Syndrome is the least common and involves the person being born sighted-hearing and losing one sense and then the other, over a period of time. They often function as a sighted-hearing individual until their hearing or sight begins to deteriorate, often in their teens, with the second loss following. Half of those who have Type 3 may have balance problems. In terms of communication difficulties, they often experience some of the same difficulties as those who have Type 2, i.e. they are not native sign language users and may need to acquire alternative communication methods as adults.

The common feature, whatever the reason for their deafblindness, is, at some point, the need for enhanced communication skills, both in themselves and in those who want to communicate with them, or who might provide interpreting or communication support. These skills can of necessity be highly specialised.

Each and every deafblind person, when their sensory loss reaches a certain level, can no longer easily communicate without special arrangements being made, and specialist skills being employed by all concerned. Hence, I have devoted the next chapter to Communication.

Chapter 5

Communication

Communicating with deafblind people involves a range of vital skills. Both the deafblind person and the communicator need to have these skills, and none of them are easily acquired. The importance of British Sign Language skills, Deafblind Manual skills, Hands-on Signing skills, Communication and Guiding skills, cannot be underestimated. Professionals working with deafblind people should ideally have all of these skills. But having them is not always enough to ensure good communication.

31: Drena O'Malley and Clark Steven

I'd like to look at communication on a higher level, when it is not only about language, or skills and qualifications – I will assume we have these – but is indeed about achieving successful communicative interactions between people, regularly and reliably and in such a way that they have access to the information they need and want.

My interest in the importance of communication was awakened when, overnight, my father lost the power of speech and of his right hand and arm, due to a stroke. I soon learned the traumatic effect of losing easy access to language, communication, and information. He continued to try to communicate using speech, most of which was unintelligible. He could not use his hand to write notes to us, and he lived for the remaining years of his life in a semi-permanent state of frustration. As a family we lived every day with a sense of helplessness. We simply couldn't fix his problem, or ours. We could not achieve successful communicative interactions regularly, reliably, or easily.

A few years later I started working for deafblind people and became further convinced of the importance of communication and linguistic access. Since I first met deafblind people in 1989 and began to learn BSL fingerspelling and Deafblind Manual, I have sought to persuade people that we should all learn alternative forms of communication, not only for the benefit of deafblind people, but for our own benefit, just in case.

Over the years I studied for and became a registered BSL interpreter as it was a great frustration that I could not communicate directly with all deaf or deafblind people, particularly those who were fully deafblind and used Hands-on Sign Language. I continue to be fascinated by the subject of communication.

The importance of communication, in all its different forms, and its impact on our human state, can pass unnoticed in our everyday lives. In 1989, as part of a Community Studies degree at Stirling University, I wrote a dissertation entitled "Falling between Two Stools" which described services to deafblind people in Scotland and how deafblind people were often fitted into services for the Deaf, or services for the

Blind, both of which often lacked the necessary specialisms in deafblindness.

In October 2002, as part of a Diploma in Sign Language Interpreting at Heriot-Watt University, I wrote a dissertation entitled "Deafblindness – the impact of sight loss on a deaf person". In the 13-year interval between these 2 pieces of writing, due to my work with deafblind people, and my abiding interest in communication and language, I came to have some understanding of the overwhelming importance to deafblind people of having successful communicative interactions. Without these they can become deprived of information with all the consequences that deprivation brings.

> "Great is language—it is the mightiest of sciences... greater than wealth... buildings, ships, religions, paintings and music" (Walt Whitman, "Poem of a Few Greatnesses")

Language acquisition is an enigma – no other system of knowledge is more easily learned at age 2 or 3 than at age 25. The language learned at home, from our parents, the language absorbed through hearing, is our first language, whether it be English or Mandarin. Without hearing, spoken language is very difficult to acquire or learn. Without hearing, sign language plays a vital role in life and learning, and will often become the first and natural language of that individual.

To the uninitiated it often seems that the quest in terms of sign language is to find a sign for each English word and then to replace a word with a sign. The problem is that spoken language is a linear sequence of sound signals, while fluent sign language is a combination of components occurring simultaneously. Sign language inevitably relies on vision, to learn it, to see it, to receive it, and to update it over time. Spoken language relies on hearing without which sound signals are little more than a pair of moving lips.

Sign language exists in every country, each of which has its own national sign language. These are languages in the same way that English, German, or French are, but deaf sign language users, unlike hearing people, can usually communicate without too much difficulty. They will also often be fluent in international sign language. I would advise hearing people who wish to learn sign language to read a little bit about Deaf culture and Deaf history before joining a class. One interesting fact to whet your appetite is that the courts of the Ottoman Empire in the 15th century employed 200 deaf sign language users. Consider that in the 21st century we have recently passed the BSL (Scotland) Act 2015 which seeks the development of a national plan to recognise and promote sign language. Sign language has been around for a very long time and is not always understood or respected in the way it should be.

There are particular benefits for deaf sign language users who use the distance sense of vision to silently access communication. This communication can happen across a table, across a football field, a hall, or busy street. Deaf sign language users can see a thought flit across the face before the thinker can hide it. Without speech, sign, or gesture the thought is read – in the raised eyebrow, quizzical expression, puckered lips, tilt of the head. Thomas Reid in his "Inquiry into the human mind" suggested that this natural language of posture and facial expression was the alphabet of humanity's first language, providing the common ground necessary for the subsequent invention and development of the arbitrary language of words. A smile, a frown, or tears are automatically understood... but only if they are seen.

Sign language is a visual language in which every movement is a performative act which communicates meaning to the observer. If the recipient blinks information can be lost. The consequences of sight loss in a deaf sign language user are therefore immense. Not only is mobility and independence threatened but their very language, and therefore the culture identified with that language. Tactile communication is useful but cannot easily convey eyebrow movements or posture, or attitude, or any other visual components of sign language. Catherine Hoffpauir Fischer in *The Orchid of the Bayou* writes:

> "Like most deaf people vision more than anything else defined my world. It was through vision that I had language and learning, vision that was sharpened by use and the need to survive. I didn't mind being deaf. Although deafness took away hearing. It gave me community – and that community was based on sight. No matter how I tried to look at it, blindness was terrifying. It was right up there with death."

Catherine has Usher Syndrome. She talks about going to school with the other kids who knew all about names. They knew about names and they used them all the time. I didn't know any names, let alone that everything I could see and touch possessed one. Her headmaster said "Catherine has to see things, what she doesn't take in with her eyes she doesn't take in at all."

The life of a deafblind person is one of constant adaptation from the time the severe dual sensory loss takes effect. Depending on age at the time of onset of the loss; the person's first language; and the primary communication method, the adaptations will be different for each individual deafblind person. Those who are Deaf sign language users, for whom the Deaf community has formed an integral part of their life, lose access not only to their language, but to their culture, and their greatest source of support. The Deaf community is often unsure how to approach those who have a dual sensory loss. Some very brave deaf individuals will just pick up the hands of a visually impaired sign language user and start signing to him/her, often in a slightly awkward fashion, as they learn which signs are more difficult to translate from being seen to being felt.

Deafblind Manual is the common currency of deafblind people, it is comparatively easy to learn to deliver, but being so reliant on English spelling, can be difficult for some. It is, however, difficult to learn to receive Deafblind Manual. Sometimes in the Deaf Club, where deafblind people should feel at home, they feel isolated. This cultural group, Deaf people, who use a beautiful expressive visual language, sometimes find it difficult to transfer to using a language based on touch and on fingerspelling. It is interesting to note that those deafblind people who meet at the Deaf Club have often formed a separate deafblind group, which is based on Hands-on Signing and Deafblind Manual – a developing Deafblind sub-culture within the Deaf community.

Language for a deafblind person, particularly one profoundly deaf from birth who uses sign language, may have taken the form of a journey on which linguistic cultural artefacts have been collected over the years. This could include English words, family signs, school signs, UK signs, Deaf Club signs, gestures learned in childhood, self-conscious signs used in teenage years, half-caught dimly seen handshapes in adulthood, and finally Hands-on Signing often introduced by a well-meaning enthusiastic skilled individual. Therefore the communication used by deafblind people is often what it needs to be for the other individual in the communicative interaction, at that time. Deafblind people's culture is to want to know that a successful exchange of information has taken place, whatever it takes to achieve that.

But what about the future? The basic qualifications which all those who work in this field or are interested in deafblindness would want to achieve have become more difficult to access, just another one of the difficulties those serving a low-incidence group have to contend with. The numbers taking deafblind qualifications are small so awarding bodies find it difficult to justify the outlay on course design, course reviews, tutor training etc. And organisations employing people in the field therefore experience greater costs.

A Diploma in Deafblind Studies was introduced in the early 2000s and I was a contributor and a tutor on the course. Almost all of the participants had significant experience and communication qualifications when they enrolled on the course so the basics were all taken care of – as they should be. Instead, I focussed on the importance of language, improving communicative interactions, raising communication to a new level, irrespective of what language or communication method was being used. I have written in the next chapter about challenges in communicating information which professionals in the field should consider. This is based on papers I have previously written and presented, aimed at BSL Interpreters, Deafblind Manual Interpreters, Guide/communicators, and other professionals. These issues remain relevant today, perhaps even more so, in an age when we almost drown in information on a daily basis.

Chapter 6

Deprivation of Information

Whatever adaptations deafblind people make, however hard they try for successful communicative interactions, they will inevitably suffer from Deprivation of Information at some points in their life. I presented a paper on this subject at a 4-day Deafblind International Conference in Leeuwenhorst in the Netherlands in June 1999 and this chapter is based on that paper.

The Deafblind International Conference also discussed the issue of translation from one language to another as being the only interpreting skill required. There were 2 distinct schools of thought at the conference. One contended that deafblind people required much more than language translation, they needed access to information and translation of that information. The other maintained that language translation could meet the need.

Incidental information

Why do I consider Deprivation of Information is inevitable for deafblind people? There are several reasons, the first of which is their inability to assimilate "incidental information" due to their having lost their "distance senses" and having to rely on "near" senses. This is information gained by looking round a room, by listening while uninvolved in a situation. It can be as simple as not knowing the number of people in a room, or the proportion of male to female, or the age groupings, whether people are attractive or ugly, well-dressed or in rags. It can be environmental information, behaviour unseen or overheard (except by a few). It is information gained, without effort, in seconds when the observer has sight and/or hearing. It is information, for example which would not normally be important enough to be given by the chairperson of a meeting or the host at an event.

Incidental information gives vital basic information but just as importantly tells us about emotions, habits, cultures, partnership possibilities, and also adds colour and flavour to life.

For example, an accent might tell us where a person originally came from, their voice might be quiet, or full of laughter, or they may be swearing or speaking in angry tones. Seeing a wedding ring might tell us their marital status, having sight might tell us who is the tallest, the youngest, the oldest person in the room. Information is all around us all the time, particularly in today's digital world. Sighted-hearing people graze on information, all day. Deafblind people receive only information which others take the time to convey to them.

It is very difficult to communicate manually "incidental information" which is normally assimilated without effort. If you sit at a meeting and focus on the incidental information you are receiving without effort, it will amaze you what you are picking up. Also give a thought as to how you might communicate that information, when, in what way, and with what importance.

Communicating all of this information, even some of it, is a real challenge and not for inexperienced guide/communicators or interpreters, but it is possible for those whose communication, paraphrasing, and hands-on skills are at a high level. Also, some deafblind people do not want to have it. They may not be used to having it, or find it is hard work to receive it, or have not had the opportunity to try receiving it.

The focus for the interpreter is always on the information being conveyed in a straightforward manner using language – whatever language is being used. The speaker will have a purpose, an aim, an opinion to convey and, understandably, this has to be interpreted in the best way possible to the deafblind person. There will often be slides, videos, questions. And it is never easy to interpret to a deafblind person, so why would interpreters worry about getting across incidental information? Perhaps with a BSL interpreter it would be possible, but if their sight is no longer good enough to see the interpreter then it's just not possible.

Inability to make sense of information received by touch

There are a number of ways to communicate by touch, all of them valid, particularly for the individual who uses that method and is comfortable with it. Fully deafblind people must necessarily rely on tactile methods of communication if they are to remain involved with society. Many adapt to Hands-on Signing when they lose vision, if BSL is their first language. However, using Hands-on Signing is a highly skilled occupation, for both parties involved, and it takes some time to develop these skills. And some information or communication is not easy to convey by touch, e.g. describing a person's ambivalent attitude, or how someone is saying one thing but obviously means another. In addition, if an interpreter uses signs with which they are unfamiliar, or is lacking skills in Hands-on Signing, or uses Deafblind Manual but has spelling difficulties, then communication can break down, information can be lost, and thus confidence affected.

Censorship

Interpreters and guide/communicators consciously and sub-consciously censor information. Families are often the main support with communication and can be reluctant to give information which they anticipate will be unpalatable, or unwelcome. Lack of vocabulary skills causes censorship. If the interpreter does not know the signs for "sacred", "Holy", "baptised" then this information may well be censored out.

Inadvertent censorship can also occur when the interpreter is just too tired, or stressed, to keep on communicating at the required level, no matter how desirable it is to do so.

Political correctness causes censorship. Deafblind Manual interpreters in training are often very reluctant to describe a person's skin colour, or height and weight etc. Similarly, everyone else in the room may be aware of relationships between people due to the behaviour exhibited, but some interpreters considered it inappropriate to tell deafblind people. Thus, they may make inappropriate advances to people. "It shouldn't be important" is a common response from interpreters. Most will admit when pressed that they initially chose their current partner based largely on decisions made using sight and hearing.

Inconsistency

Interpreters can give information to all different levels, some go into a lot of detail, others very little; guide/communicators can offer a number of different options, or none; some will sit down and launch into communicating without any consultation. It is important to know what is important to the individual. Lexicon can be important, in that family signs can be a boon, giving a shorthand way of communicating. But equally family signs can act to disadvantage deafblind people if they don't understand more widely used signs.

Colour and flavour

Incidental information has its rightful place in providing colour and flavour to the information being interpreted to the deafblind person. The confident deafblind person may tell the interpreter "I've heard all this before, just let me know who is here that I might know." Most won't. They may come to dread meetings where speakers feel they have to give all the information they researched, not thinking it might be difficult to receive without access to graphs, pictures, and other interesting asides.

Incidental information can be the item of most interest that day. Many years ago, at the end of a SAGOD meeting a deafblind person came to me and said "I hear you've dyed your hair a different colour, and it doesn't suit you." I laughed and replied "We've trained that guide well, if you've been told that. And I don't like it either!" I asked what she thought of the 5-year plan we were discussing and she commented on 2 items which reassured me she was getting the information she needed.

Long-term effects of Deprivation of Information

Deprivation of Information creates long-term effects on deafblind individuals. They make poor decisions based on poor information and can lose confidence in their ability to access accurate information or make accurate assessments. Learning new skills, being updated, getting the news becomes more difficult, which can lead to out-of-date views and attitudes. Today's fully deafblind people are a particular example of that cumulative effect. If a person has been fully deafblind for 20 years, they may be almost totally unaware of the equality agenda and legislation, political correctness, social media etc. And even the changes in the way women live their lives. Unless they receive specific training, they can stumble on inadvertently causing offence without realising it, or being ostracised for their actions, giving them yet another reason to become withdrawn, and generally stay at home.

The stages of Deprivation of Information were categorised in my paper as deafblind people becoming: Disaffected, Disappointed, Disengaged, and finally Disappeared from everyday life. Being informed, having access to information of all kinds, can be so much hard work that it's just not worth the effort. We have to make it easy for them to access as much as they can. They need regular breaks, comfortable seats for both deafblind person and interpreter, opportunities to communicate directly with others, they need to know who is present, and as much incidental information as might interest them.

Dr T.R. Armitage, founder of the British and Foreign Blind Association many years ago, summed it up so much better than I can when he said:

> "A man is isolated by everything which renders the acquisition of knowledge difficult and tedious.... And his isolation is diminished by everything which facilitates his power of self-education." (1886)

Deafblind culture

When we think of language and communication there are always cultural issues and I was inspired a number of years ago to research the question "If there is a Deaf culture, is there in a similar way, a Deafblind culture, or sub-culture?" While Deaf culture is a subject of interest, little has been written about the emergence of Deafblind culture.

Very briefly, I found that within the Deafblind world there exists a culture which has much to do with Deprivation of Information stemming from receiving poor-quality information. They develop behaviours, coping strategies to deal with the constant doubt which permeates their lives. And these behaviours are assimilated by others. This can involve a range of tactics, as follows.

They often use **Repetition**, e.g. they seek reassurance from a number of people, on a number of levels and a number of times seeking to ensure they have the right information.

They seek **Confirmation**, e.g. when a piece of information gleaned by whatever means from one person is over a period checked out with several others.

They **Share Information** – in a similar way to Deaf people sharing information, deafblind people often share information, thus demonstrating how important knowledge is to them. Information is power.

They often **Control the Conversation**. If a deafblind person controls the conversation, they know what the subject matter is. Difficulties can arise when a sighted-hearing person introduces a new topic leaving the deafblind person behind. Hence controlling the conversation is a very effective way of the deafblind person knowing what is being said. They lead the conversation. They ask questions, often of a personal nature, of people, or about people. For them it is all just information, and we should see it that way. Armitage's quote is helpful in that regard.

Pursuing activities with other deafblind people. They often prefer operating in what might be described in some circles as a deafblind "ghetto" to mainstream activities as it is easier to interact with others in their community, where difficulty with language, communication, information is not only an everyday occurrence but an hourly one. It is not a ghetto, nurses often spend time with other nurses, teachers similarly. It is part of their culture to be with others with whom communication is easier.

The subject of communication and language as it affects deafblind people is indeed a fascinating one which I can only cover briefly in this chapter. There is much we can do to improve things for deafblind people if we simply consider the difficulties they face and do 4 things – improve the skills and knowledge of the Language Service Professionals who provide their communication services, develop new skills around paraphrasing, recognise the importance of assimilated information, and do everything possible to prevent Deprivation of Information. Once deprivation has occurred it becomes the norm and the rot sets in. All of us need to have our thinking and our practice challenged if we are to improve the situation for deafblind people.

Chapter 7

The Importance of Painting the Full Picture for deafblind people

This subject matter flowed from the concept discussed at the conference in the Netherlands that "deafblind people require much more than language translation, they need information translation".

In 2004 I presented a paper to BSL Interpreters on how to include deafblind people in conferences. "Painting the Full Picture" involves using a set of principles to guide how we might translate and convey information for deafblind people, both when using language in real time or conveying information in written form or alternative formats.

The principles and tactics suggested here remain relevant, hence I have included it in this section about communication. The aim is to reduce the effort deafblind people need to make to access information and communication which is available to other participants. My aim was to give guide/communicators and other Language Service Professionals principles and tactics which would help them to both interpret language and information, and also to achieve successful communicative interactions.

Experienced guide/communicators have a wealth of experience in achieving successful interactions between deafblind people and others, no matter what the difficulties are. This is sometimes called "Plugging the Gap". Wherever a communication breakdown occurs with any regularity, guide/communicators will identify it as a “gap” and work out how it can be plugged.

During the 1998 World Cup, when deafblind men wanted access to information it was agreed one way to provide access to football games might be to use the person’s hand not only to receive Deafblind Manual, but as the pitch, with the guide/communicator’s forefinger as the ball. This method of communicating a match was successfully tried and that particular gap was filled for one individual. And then it was offered to others, some of whom liked it and used it regularly. However, others reverted to receiving an account of the game in Moon or Braille a few days later.

A strategy of “Plugging the Gap” often works. If an individual wants to learn karate, the guides work out with the individual how to convey the information, which might be the best signs to use, in what situation, how best to deliver them. And then this information is shared with other Language Service Professionals (LSPs), and reviewed and developed over time. The **first principle** of Painting the Full Picture is:

Life contains many facets, and all of them should be communicable, given sufficient language skills, time, effort, and imagination.

There was, however, always a school of thought which believed that if LSPs develop the communication skills and qualifications necessary to interpret and deliver information, that should meet the needs of deafblind people. If they had a professional attitude, followed a professional Code of Practice, prepared for assignments, and religiously translated spoken or written English into BSL or Deafblind Manual, then surely their job was done? What more was needed?

We have already looked at some length at the importance that incidental information can hold for all of us, and the need for deafblind people in particular to have access to it, or at least some of it. This non-verbal, sometimes non-language information is often deemed to be less important than verbal or linguistic information A **second principle** is that:

Whatever information is available to sighted-hearing people should be made available to deafblind people, as and when the opportunity permits, in a simple, but informative way, without censorship.

Without the information provided by our distance senses information can become simply a string of words or signs, at best soundbites. At a conference for example, others are looking at slides while listening to the words associated with that slide. This simple visual aid helps give shape to the speech. A structure in which the interpreted information can be conveyed to the deafblind person is similarly critical to the understanding of the message.

It is important to remember that if a guide/communicator interprets only the words on a slide then the person receives only soundbites of information. Similarly, if the LSP interprets only some of the spoken word in order of utterance then the concept of the main points and how the theme was developed may be lost.

When providing training on this subject I tell a true story of my own experience in a toilet cubicle when I can hear a very interesting conversation outside the cubicle, all in Glasgow vernacular. As an example, the following discourse was part of it:

> "So Ah come in an' he's like this. So Ah'm like that. Ma sister's like this. So he was like that. "Whaur dae ye think ye're gaun?" Nane o' your frigging business. Ma sister's like this. Next thing he's like that. Ends up."
> "Aw naw! Aw ower the carpet?"
> "Aye. Ah wis like that."

I came out of the cubicle too late to find out what was all over the carpet – vomit, blood, a Chinese sweet and sour chicken. I was left wanting to know more. Language on its own hadn't worked for me. They may not have used BSL, but they had certainly used a visual, gestural language, which, in the circumstances, was not available to me behind a door!

We need to be more aware of how many aspects there are to achieving full access to information and full access to communication. A **third principle** is that:

We all receive information in context, a context most often picked up by our eyes and ears.

Sometimes the context is the History, the Geography, even the Relationships. The "soundbite" culture mitigates against "Painting the Full Picture". Be aware of a **fourth principle**:

Painting the Full Picture doesn't mean giving more information. It does mean giving clearer,

paraphrased information, as part of a framework which helps provide the context.

When we try to piece together a jigsaw most of us proceed in an orderly manner. We don't just see 2 pieces in the same colour and try to put them together. We set up the corners. We look for pieces which form the 4 sides and we work at building the frame. We do this before we can begin to make sense of the jigsaw. Taking a similar approach can be vital to the receipt of interpreted information. The picture on the box is to the jigsaw what the context is to interpreted information.

For example, be clear about the

WHEN what's the timeline, when did/will it happen?
WHO is speaking, or who is the leading character?
WHERE is the action happening/where will be affected?
WHY is it important?
WHAT is the purpose of the speech/event?
Most information, events, meetings, conferences, stories contain the above 5 elements which can help give shape and form to interpretation. The type of clarity used in BSL grammatical structure can be of assistance in trying to paint a full picture, e.g. in a BSL conversation we tend to expect information on the timeline or the topic to come first. Snap judgements sometimes have to be made in deciding what we can and cannot convey. And we cannot always give all the information we might like to. Indeed, the deafblind person might not want it. Ask them how much they know about it, or indeed want to know.

The final and **fifth principle** is that:

The Context is essential – to painting the full picture, to telling the story, to facilitating a meaningful communicative interaction which meets the needs of all parties involved.

For deafblind people you as a communicator should strive to create a good framework, and involve deafblind people in a story which makes sense to them and is understandable.

Skilled paraphrasing is required if we are not to descend into soundbites of unconnected information. If we have created a structure or framework we can refer back to it, we can continue the story. Because in the end all information tells a story.

Preparation is key. Research the information to be conveyed, who the participants are, acquire a programme, an agenda, any papers or presentations to be used, and handouts. Ask the questions you need to know. It is impossible to paraphrase information into Deafblind Manual without this information. It is very difficult to paint any kind of meaningful picture without this information.

Bert Riedel

For those who don't yet have the alternative communication skills which they might need I want to end this section on communication with the story of Bert Riedel.

Bert Riedel started to study sign language when he was 86 years old and already fully deafblind. He had moved in with his daughter and her family and communication was far from easy. He had Usher Syndrome type 3 meaning he was born with sight and hearing and steadily lost his sight first, followed by his hearing, which meant he had speech. When Diane Chambers, who was an American Sign Language interpreter, was moved to help him learn to sign, she went to meet him to find him playing Beethoven on his piano, from memory.

His main way of communicating was via a Braille machine, which was very heavy. But in order to part in family gatherings or events the Braille machine was lugged round so he could feel what was happening in Braille and respond accordingly using speech.

There were many setbacks, but after a full year of teaching and practising, one day Bert said "I was run down from 40 years of pretending to be like everybody else when I couldn't hear or see. Now with interpreters like you I'm getting what I never had before. When you sign to me I can hear the words in my head like you are talking to me." That was indeed a great day for his tutor. Over 2 years they worked on, meeting weekly. Many life events got in the way, but they persisted. And other sign language users also practised with Bert whenever they could.

Diane asked Bert one day how he felt about Helen Keller's quote "Blindness cuts people off from things, but deafness cuts people off from people."

Bert responded:

> "People can live without sight. When I lost my sight I listened to "The Rise and the Fall of the Roman Empire". I loved it. I had talking books, I had friends, and I had my music... Blind people can potentiate their hearing and their

smell. They can recognise people by their walk or by their scent or their voice... I think sound is the most beautiful sense in our body.

For me, sound is preferable to sight for joy in my life. I miss hearing a child's voice... and I miss conversation. And now without my hearing or my sight I miss the life I was part of.

But when you give the gift of sign language to a deafblind old man, that's life! It's like a mother giving birth to a child! I was scared of sign language in the beginning. Now I look forward to our sign talk. When understanding flows, you have real life."

That is the truth about communication. When understanding flows, however it is achieved, you have real life. It is never too late to find a way to have successful communicative interactions, on both sides. It is never too late to have a real life. Bert lived for several more years, comfortably communicating in fingerspelling and tactile sign language with anyone who could use it.

(Information on the Bert Riedel story was taken from *Words in My Hands* by Diane Chambers, Ellexa Press LLC, 2012.)

Conclusion

For deafblind people communication is an ongoing journey of adaptation, and thus it should be also for those privileged to join them on that journey.

Chapter 8

"Influencing"

The phrase sometimes used to describe the impact that NDBL Scottish office had in its early days was "punching above our weight". We tended to choose issues and campaigns carefully as we were aware of our size and our limited resources. Sometimes we responded to an opportunity which was presented when we were invited to comment on a report, or proposed legislation, or to take part in consultation, or to join a strategy group.

However, "influencing" in terms of deafblind people might bring to mind a picture of an individual with a problem visiting their local councillor, or even a Community Council meeting, or their MSP in the Scottish Parliament, or writing to a newspaper, or getting a petition together. These actions would be considered normal for an individual or group striving to improve things, fighting an injustice, seeking a fairer outcome. But when a deafblind person is striving for change, they face endemic problems when they want to meet an MSP, or a councillor, or attend a meeting. They need communication support to be able to do so. They need guide/communicator support to be able to travel to a venue. They find it very difficult, or impossible to communicate by email. It requires such an effort on the part of deafblind people to seek change, or even influence, so when they take a step forward in a political sense it is cause for celebration. It is also daunting for them when they fail to gain support for some changes which seem to them to be a no-brainer.

Deafblindness is a low-incidence disability, about which little is known by the general public, the government, or politicians. The biggest challenge deafblind people face is to get their needs, particularly their needs regarding communication, on to the political agenda. This chapter tells the story of their efforts to affect that agenda, to have their needs recognised, and considered – when legislation, guidance, benefits changes are being developed.

32: NDBL's Aberdeen group, early 1950s

The NDBL was already operating in Scotland in the early 1950s. There was a thriving group of deafblind people in Aberdeen and there is an impressive picture of NDBL's Aberdeen Group on an outing to Huntly in September 1957. Pictured second from the right is Mrs Evelyn Nicol, The League's energetic Steward in Aberdeen.

The League produced regular newsletters and in June 1952 one was produced under the title "News, Notes, and Notices" which describes 6 members and 3 associates enjoying a pleasant social evening in the Royal Blind Association canteen, Edinburgh: "The monthly tea meetings now given for the deaf-blind in Edinburgh and surrounding districts by Mr Cormack, Supt, and his home teachers, are very much appreciated."

The *Rainbow* magazine was a real lifeline for many deafblind people in the early days, offering a way of keeping in touch with each other, and also provided in alternative formats when this became possible. Nan Love, Bella Moran, Dorrie Moore, and Mary McInnes all from the Glasgow area were regular contributors to the *Rainbow*. They succeeded in meeting in person at outings and events, particularly at the annual rally in Peterborough. Most came into contact with each other and with NDBL during their working lives in workshops for the blind and they maintained contact with deafblind people throughout the UK via *Rainbow* magazine. I have a memory of Dorrie, Bella, and Nan sitting in a row at a meeting in Glasgow communicating in Deafblind Manual all at the same time, with the hands of all 3 working simultaneously to give and receive information.

This group began to develop connections with deafblind people in other countries, possibly due to international events happening in the UK. As they did so, they learned what was happening in other countries. For example, in Scandinavia people had the services of a Contact Person to take them to meetings etc. and provide communication support. In the USA people were learning sign language in ever increasing numbers and they were becoming interpreters for deaf people, with some beginning to provide services to deafblind people.

Then, when I came into post, I could see they now harboured notions of not only having a social life – although they always enjoyed a Deafblind Manual blether – but they now hoped they might emulate what was beginning to happen in other countries, often in the wake of better services, as a right, for the Deaf community.

33:Anne Barnett ,Wendy Forrest, Drena O'Malley, John Frame, Ellen Cattanach, 1994

A presence in Scotland was needed if Scottish deafblind people were to be able to use their influence, and NDBL responded to members' request for a worker in Scotland. And I came along to fill that post. But NDBL did more than that, within months Ann Barnett had agreed that any funds raised in Scotland could be spent in Scotland so we could develop quickly. Ellen Cattanach was employed part-time within months in an administrative role so that I could spend my time meeting deafblind people and developing services for them. And soon after Wendy Forrest joined us with a view to raising our profile and also much-needed funds.

In the early days of NDBL operating in Scotland some progress was made in having deafblind people's needs recognised due to the "Breaking Through" Report of 1988 being published, which was the first report to focus solely on deafblindness. It viewed deafblindness as a separate and unique disability and brought a profile to deafblindness never previously enjoyed. As such, it attracted attention. I had written 2 papers on deafblindness for Stirling University, and these could be supplementary for those who were interested in a Scottish perspective. There was little else at that time available on acquired deafblindness. The attention that the "Breaking Through" report generated created opportunities for deafblind people to meet the decision-makers, and they enthusiastically embraced these opportunities to tell people about their life experiences, the difficulties they encounter, the problems they have to overcome. Without that report "Influencing" would not have happened the way it did over a period of 25 years.

At the same time as "Breaking Through" came onto the agenda, 3 women were quietly building a relationship, beginning to work together and to campaign, especially where there were opportunities to benefit all deafblind people. So not only did we have Gill Morbey of Sense Scotland and I working together, more able to represent the needs of all ages of deafblind people, we had Dorrie Moore, who was able to represent her own needs and those of all fully deafblind adults very eloquently. In terms of deafblindness – it was a perfect storm.

Dorrie Moore was a past master when meeting people. She would not easily be silenced; she would not be made to fit in with any given situation. Dorrie could hear nothing, see nothing and used Deafblind Manual to communicate. I often acted as her guide and rarely advised her not to speak. She would often make a point when she remembered it, unaware of who else was speaking at the time. She interrupted, on one occasion, Archbishop Winning and on another, Prince Phillip. I was with her on both occasions and It was a small but enlightening moment for people when they realised that fully deafblind people really can't see or hear what is happening, can't hear conversation going on around them. Dorrie was unusual in that she had confidence in her ability to communicate. Others didn't. Other deafblind people often kept quiet for fear of interrupting those conversations, and, unless a skilled guide/communicator enabled them to participate, their point was often not put across.

Dorrie had advocated to NDBL for many years that Scottish members should have their own Liaison Officer, based in Glasgow. So my appointment was a good example of deafblind people using influence to achieve an aim. Dorrie in particular simply lobbied the NDBL Board. Scottish deafblind people very much wanted a greater say in how The League operated in Scotland, and to influence activities in Scotland.

Without regular and automatic access to skilled professional communication support deafblind people can live a life of splendid isolation, unable to participate, unable to influence anything that happens in their lives. The saddest sight in my working life – and it happened all too often – was to see a deafblind person, who obviously had something to say, not being enabled to make their point. Because that sort of exclusion becomes a learned way of life.

In 1994 we purchased a small retail shop in Lenzie. Ann Barnett considered having car parking nearby and being near a railway station were high on the list of desirable features for a new office. This was our first purchase of property and was not to be our last. NDBL funded the purchase and the Scottish office agreed to fundraise to replace the funds used, when and if it

34: Anne Barnett with Dorrie Moore cutting the ribbon at the opening of 21 Alexandra Avenue

were possible. We put in heating, did some renovations and put Scottish Rainbow on the window.

One of my main ambitions was to have deafblind people influence everything that affects them, goes on around them, or impacts on their quality of life. Now that they had a Liaison Officer and a small number of Scottish members had a guide/communicator service the opportunity was there. They needed to get "out there" and let others know they were able to participate, given communication support. Therefore any vehicle which would facilitate their being involved and able to influence was to be welcomed. And the first vehicle to present was a Forum on Deafblindness in 1992 and the second, which has served deafblind people well since its inception, was the Scottish Advisory Group on Deafblindness. The next chapters tell the story of why and how deafblind people were able to influence – or not as the case may be – outcomes which affected their lives.

Chapter 9

"Influencing"

The Annual Forum on Deafblindness

The Scottish Advisory Group on Deafblindness

Inspired by the approach taken by the leadership within NDBL I was very keen that the fast-growing group of members within Scotland felt they had a real say in what happened not only within the organisation in Scotland, but also in the national organisation and in decisions made in the wider community which may affect them. I was also keen members had a real sense of ownership of the organisation which seeks to serve them.

35: Sanja Tarczay at the Forum, 2004 at the Golden Lion, Stirling

Forum on Deafblindness 1992-2007

A great example of what deafblind people can do was set when the first Forum on Deafblindness took place in June 1992. Led by the example set by Dottie Entwhistle and Patrick Murphy deafblind people spoke from the front. Sarah Reed, John Dearie, and Evelyn

Brown spoke about the Usher Syndrome Support Group to invited councillors, politicians, and workers in the field. There were workshops on offer, some led by deafblind people, some by organisations in the field, all offering opportunities to learn. Central Region Social Work department spoke about their guide-help scheme, Sense Scotland spoke about their Family Centre, CACDP gave an update on available qualifications, and Barrowfield Deaf-blind Complex about the opportunities for supported housing.

The Forums continued annually until 2007, one day a year when the focus was on deafblindness, and workers, politicians, and families gathered to learn about new developments within the field, and to hear from the deafblind speakers. Deafblind people were there in number to hear directly from experts in the field, and to hear from other deafblind people who were experts on the subject of deafblindness. The Forums were held in Edinburgh, Dundee, Perth, Stirling, and Glasgow.

A number of very well-known speakers took part in them including John Bishop, SWSI; Jean Maclellan, Scottish executive; Mary Mulligan, Deputy Minister for Health and Community Care; Bette Francis, ASP Unit; Sanja Tarczay from Croatia; Danny Delcambre, USA; and Ove Bejsnap from Denmark. Donald Dewar was booked to speak, but his flight was late and he arrived as the deafblind people were leaving the building. He invited them back into the Assembly rooms in George Street, Edinburgh and held court for a further hour which greatly impressed those who met him.

In 1997 it was considered essential to increase the input of Scottish deafblind members to the decision-making processes which were affecting their lives. A group of people met on 20 November 1997 in the first meeting of the Scottish Advisory Group on Deafblindness (SAGOD). This meeting was held in Tom Johnson House, Kirkintilloch with members coming from all over Scotland. They wanted to influence what was happening in their lives and agreed the way to do it was to arrange a regular physical meeting of deafblind people supported by appropriate communication support where Scottish deafblind people could discuss with each other a plan of action to achieve their objectives. DBUK's constitutional aim was wholly acceptable as the main objective for the group. "To further the interests of deafblind persons by every means and in every way open to it. Deafblind should include those substantially deprived of sight and hearing."

The aims of the group were agreed as:

- To improve the lives of deafblind people within Scotland by seeking to influence policy at every level – government, local authority, service-providers and society in general.
- To assist deafblind people gain the information, training and experience to enable them to achieve the above aims for themselves.
- To inform policy within Deafblind UK regarding the organisation's work in Scotland.

A group of 15–20 people met quarterly in different cities and towns and discussed a whole range of issues, planning and taking action on a number of them. Local MPs, councillors, social workers, were invited to attend and interact with deafblind people.

However, they were discouraged from making speeches, rather our elected representatives were invited to hear from deafblind people. Achieving a guide/communicator service for every deafblind people who needs it was then a standing agenda item for SAGOD. They discussed every major report issued which might impact upon them. And they agreed which issues to take forward to their MP or mount a campaign about. Occasionally over the years they pointed out failings within the organisation which I was charged with improving. To my mind this served only to show that SAGOD was effective.

SAGOD meetings were slightly chaotic. Tactile communication users need to be together in the same place to be in contact with others, so the first hour was spent saying hello to others. This was one of only a handful of opportunities to do that each year. The agenda was less important than that vital connection person to person. However, as they continued to regularly meet, their agenda developed and this comparatively small group of deafblind people, over a period of 10 years, either contributed to, played a major part in achieving, or commissioned The League in Scotland to achieve for them:

- A guide/communicator service for every deafblind person who needs it
- Section 7 Guidance to be implemented in Scotland
- The Scottish Office to become a separate Scottish charity
- A new centre for deafblind people to be acquired

- Linguistic access for all deafblind people via a Sign Language Act
- The development of training for the guide/communicators
- Free rail travel for the guide/communicator or family member accompanying a deafblind person to travel by rail
- Deafblindness to be treated as a separate disability in government reports
- The development of Scottish Executive Data Standards for dual sensory impairment.

I have told the story throughout the following chapters of how the top 6 aims came about, were achieved, or failed to materialise. While I believe that there was an element of good or bad luck in the outcome for each of them, a great deal of time, effort, and persistence was spent by deafblind people in trying to achieve these aims. They made representation, on other issues too. Several of the aims have not yet been realised, one of them being Section 7 Guidance being implemented in Scotland.

Chapter 10

"Influencing" -The development of the Deafblind Studies Diploma

36: Deafblind Studies Diploma Group at graduation, 2004

In the late 1990s, as the guide/communicator service began to develop, the guides began to acquire qualifications in communication and language skills, mainly in BSL. There was a CACDP (Council for the Advancement of Communication with Deaf People, now known as Signature) qualification in Communicating and Guiding with Deafblind People and we put hundreds of guides and potential guides through it. The service was becoming recognised as a specialist one.

Over time it became apparent that the range of qualifications in deafblindness was incomplete, especially at the higher levels. Deafblind people were aware that great effort was going into training and developing BSL interpreting services and were keen that guide/communicators should have access to training in skills, including BSL skills. I was eager to ensure that guide/communicators could progress their skills level in the same way as BSL interpreters had succeeded in doing.

In 1997, at a meeting of the Deafblind Services Liaison Group, Roy Lawrenson, of the Guide Dogs for the Blind Association's School of Rehabilitation Studies, was asked to invite interested parties to a workshop on developing high-level training in deafblindness. It was initially suggested that this could possibly form part of a GDBA Rehabilitation course. Jackie Scott, the chief executive of DBUK, asked me to attend as the DBUK representative. Others invited were Bob Peckford of CACDP, Liz Booth of Sense Scotland, Virginia Von Malachowski, Norman Brown, Alison Bennett, Graham Hicks and Mary Guest from Sense Scotland, Julie Brown of Deafblind UK, Simon Eamonson, Tom Muldowney, and Alan Sloman of GDBA. This list of invitees comes from a minute of meeting and I think it is interesting to see how the great and the good from that period were all keen to see this qualification come about. Indeed, the Deafblind Services Liaison Group was responsible for so many advances made at that time for deafblind people.

I met with Tom Muldowney in Glasgow, and then in October 1997 a meeting finally took place when GDBA, DBUK, Sense UK, and CACDP, met in Hindhead, Surrey, to discuss the need for a specialist qualification in Deafblindness. The main items to be discussed at a meeting were (1) the viability of a deafblind module or qualification, (2) the content of the modules, and (3) the putting together of a project team. At that meeting it was agreed that a professional qualification was needed, containing various modules. Just adding a module to the GDBA Rehabilitation course would not meet the need. Over the next 5 years slowly but surely, modules were developed, improved, and added to by a group of experts in the field who gave their time voluntarily to develop a course. From the beginning it was agreed that the course would cover the needs of both congenital and acquired deafblindness. This was a major challenge but a great principle to work from.

As is often the case in small organisations, if they want to see change, they have to roll up their sleeves and make that change happen. Virginia Von Malachowski took the lead in order to progress the project. The universities of Edinburgh and Birmingham, and finally the Open University, were involved in validating the course over the following years. In 2002 the efforts of that initial group were rewarded when tranche 1 of a new Diploma in Deafblind Studies was launched. This was a 2-year course with a certificate awarded on successful completion of the first year of the course. Participants had to have qualifications in communications skills prior to achieving the Diploma. The course, its content, and its effectiveness were continually monitored and every year one module was reviewed and updated. Since 2002 dozens of students from all over UK and abroad have achieved this specialist diploma, bringing a new professionalism to workers in the field of deafblindness. Deafblind Scotland put most staff on the course and many of the guide/communicators, particularly senior guides. Sense UK did the same. The other sensory impairment organisations could provide fewer students as they had fewer staff actually hands-on working with deafblind people.

At that time Signature (formerly known as CACDP) provided qualifications in British Sign Language, Deafblind Manual Interpreting, Communication and

Guiding Skills with Deafblind people, and Interpreting in both BSL and Deafblind Manual. There was now a qualifications framework for professionals working with deafblind people. Deafblind Scotland was involved in the development of these deafblind qualifications.

There were inherent difficulties in providing a course at Diploma level for people working in a low-incidence disability. I had favoured using the NVQ/SVQ route to make it more affordable, but a university-approved qualification was the desired and agreed option. The Diploma modules and its delivery mode continued to adapt to changing times and later it was delivered online. The heyday of the course was from 2002 to 2014 and then demand began to slow. It was then agreed to put the course into cold storage for a time. However, I am keen to see it in operation again in some way. It was a dynamic qualification which continued to change and adapt to the needs of the professionals both in terms of content, the shape of the course, the delivery mode, and the awarding body, and therein lay its strength. At the time of writing, I believe there are moves afoot to reinstate the Diploma, and that would be very welcome news.

Chapter 11

"Influencing" - The guide/communicator service

The development of a guide/communicator service, and their being able to access a service was of the utmost importance to most deafblind people and remains a major agenda item for them to this day. Hence, they sought to use their influence to bring it about, to improve it, and to expand it throughout Scotland.

The guide/communicator service became a priority for me within weeks of beginning work for the NDBL, and reading the "Breaking Through" report which stated that "life for a deafblind person is significantly enriched if a guide/help service is available". My research then showed that Scandinavia was the example to follow for services to deafblind people.

The effect of the "Breaking Through" report and a new NDBL office in Scotland was that by July 1990 I was already meeting with Social Work departments to try to persuade them to provide a guide/help service for deafblind people, similar to that available in Scandinavian countries. The early 1990s was a halcyon time for deafblindness when people began to become aware of deafblind people's needs, particularly their need for a guide/communicator service. They recognised this as the key to enabling deafblind people to lead useful and fulfilling lives.

There were a number of highly significant events in the early 1990s which helped to put deafblindness on the map. Most of the credit for this must go to staff in Peterborough who sought to capitalise on now having a presence in Scotland.

In April 1990 NDBL held a training course in Communication with Deaf-blind persons over 6 evenings in Glasgow & West of Scotland Society for the Deaf, Norfolk Street, Glasgow. Tutors included Richard James, June Brooks, Dottie Entwhistle (deafblind), Patrick Murphy (deafblind), and me. The centre was full with almost 50 people taking part in the course and all the necessary communication support personnel accompanying them. Social workers, health workers, BSL interpreters, and lots of workers in the field came along. This sort of training was hitherto unknown in Scotland and it helped Stewart Simpson of CACDP to decide that Scotland was the place for them to roll out new qualifications for those working with deafblind people. And that decision alone led to essential qualifications for guide/communicators being available in Scotland.

Within weeks "The Way Ahead" Seminar was held in the Central Hotel, Glasgow. There were various speakers including Patrick Murphy as representative of the European Federation of the Blind; Professor Fred Edwards who spoke on "Breaking Through"; Dorrie Moore who spoke about her life experiences; and Gill Morbey, Bob Winter, and I who spoke on the services needed by deafblind people, and those currently being provided. There was a discussion with a panel of 4 on the theme "The Way Ahead". Forty deafblind people attended, together with the same number of workers in the field. This was the moment when the great and the good of Glasgow met deafblind people in numbers for the first time and they were amazed by the different communication methods used, and the views expressed. This was also the inspiration for NDBL in Scotland to initiate an annual Forum on Deafblindness in Scotland, one day a year when workers and deafblind people could attend a conference which was dedicated to deafblindness and to having deafblind speakers.

These 2 very unusual events, entirely focussed on deafblindness and happening within weeks of each other, were the ideal launch for the new Scottish operation, and since Peterborough staff did most of the work it was manna from heaven.

A year later NDBL Peterborough hosted an international convention in Edinburgh in which more than 100 deafblind people and their guides took part. There were speakers from all over the world and I was certainly amazed at how most speakers were deafblind people themselves. I have no doubt these events very much shaped my approach when I saw for myself what could be done.

Review of Services for the Deaf

In 1991/2 there was a review into services for the Deaf in Strathclyde Regional Council. This was later expanded to include deafblind people after we facilitated deafblind people to meet the movers and shakers in Strathclyde Regional Council. When people in power are exposed to deafblind people using tactile communication with each other and with guide/communicators then the penny drops that life is incredibly difficult even with a skilled guide/communicator in place.

The 24-page review of service to deafblind people was published by Strathclyde Regional Council, having been worked on by Alex McPherson, Coordinator Services for the Deaf, and Cath Simpson, Coordinator Services for the Blind, and followed the same format as the Deaf review. It was a watershed moment that a separate review of services to deafblind people was thought necessary, and was undoubtedly due in part to the increasing profile of deafblindness in Scotland.

The Review recommended that

> "for those deaf-blind people living in the community, a guide-help or guide-interpreter scheme could dramatically improve the quality of life. A few hours a week from a guide-help can allow the deaf-blind person to integrate in normal activities such as shopping, swimming, visiting friends, placing a bet or going to the pub. This can have a very positive effect as has been witnessed... A guide-help scheme would be a very effective use of resources."

Two weeks later Phil Bryers, Assistant Director, Adult Care, invited me to a meeting with him and Fred Edwards to discuss my dissertation on deafblindness which I had produced for Stirling University. It was a positive meeting where deafblind people's need for a guide/communicator service was discussed in some depth. However, a major question was who would provide the service. In September I wrote to him to confirm that the provision of a guide/communicator service was within the capabilities of NDBL in Scotland and we would be happy to develop and provide a specialist service. NDBL in Peterborough were supportive of this, which was far-sighted to say the least.

Preparing the way for a guide/communicator service

In 1993, 120 members local to Strathclyde Region had been consulted as to how they might use a guide/communicator service and they were full of ideas. In June 1993, the "Out of Touch" report was released by NDBL in Scotland. This report showed that 40% of deafblind people had to use 2 methods of communication at the same time to get information, e.g. lip-reading and BSL; it was not a simple case of using BSL or lip-reading or clear speech. The report also found that the average length of time for which people experienced a severe dual sensory loss was 24 years, so this was not only a problem of old age.

Strathclyde Regional Council then considered various ways of providing an in-house guide/communicator service including training existing home-helps in communication skills, with a view to them taking on extra hours. The lack of communication skills was immediately a real and present problem for both parties. It was also totally impractical to train BSL interpreters so that they could fulfil the guide/communicator role as there were too few. This approach of locating services to deafblind people within bigger, less-specialised services has tended to continue to the present day, and is understandable, but with specialist communication skills as a major requirement, it simply doesn't work, perhaps because it is always more complicated to work with the dual loss, rather than a single loss. I was not particularly keen to build a new service, with all that that entailed, but I was keen for a service to be started. There really was no choice.

In 1994/95 in-depth discussions took place on training and using specialist guide/communicators to provide a small service within Strathclyde Region. In December 1994 Ann Davis, service manager for Strathclyde Regional Sign Language Interpreting Service (RSLIS) and I met to agree ground rules for such a service. During February and March 1995, the Service Level Agreement was discussed at length and agreed between Alex McPherson of Strathclyde Regional Council and The League in Scotland.

An agency agreement

This Agency agreement — the first of its kind — between Strathclyde Regional Council and NDBL's Scottish office was finally agreed and signed on 22 February 1995 for the provision of a guide/communicator service. It was agreed that:

> "The Communicator/guide will be qualified and experienced as agreed by the RSLIS. The Communicator/guide service will provide users access to wider services and provide greater participation and integration in the community through appropriate communication support. This support must be independent, confidential and accountable, working within the RSLIS Code of Practice and the agreed complaints procedure. The Social

> Work Committee expects NDBL will provide up to 24.5 hours per week sessional Communicator/guide support at £8.20 per hour and provide this service to a minimum of 5 deafblind people per week."

Potential guide/communicators were interviewed in April 1995, £5000 funding was received from Strathclyde Regional Council's BSL interpreting budget to enable training, and in May 1995 the service was implemented using 3 guides, John Frame, Jim Tracy, and Janet Gilroy, 2 of whom were already excellent signers when they came to us. The agreement required the guide/communicators to be qualified in CACDP Communication and Guiding Skills with deafblind people and to have achieved or be working towards BSL Level 2. It also required guide/communicators to have a job description, and to abide by a code of ethics similar to that used by Strathclyde Region's BSL interpreters.

Putting the case for a guide/communicator service throughout Scotland

The Scottish Office Home and Health Department was persuaded by an application in 1995 to provide Section 10 funding for 3 years to promote the development of a guide/communicator service across Scotland. Meetings took place with existing regional authorities and again with new local authorities when the regions were divided in 1996. Seminars where deafblind people spoke about their needs were held in all parts of Scotland. And local authorities and health boards began to recognise that the guide/communicator service is essential if deafblind people are to be involved in any meaningful way in their communities. The service began to grow and spread throughout Scotland.

In the meantime, we were adding potential guide/communicators to the payroll as we went along, having trained them in small groups. Similarly, deafblind people were being added as service-users, one at a time. The amount of need we identified within the deafblind population at that time was substantial, and much of it was both unknown and urgent. It fell to Deafblind Scotland to try to arrange a way to have these needs met, often by persuading local authorities to get involved.

Progressing in parallel was our campaign to have a guide/communicator service provided in medical settings, and on 6 February 1998 the MEL (1998)4 was issued by the Department of Health. This required all health boards and NHS trusts to ensure that deafblind people are afforded the services of a guide/communicator when they attend hospital or a GP surgery. This was a major achievement for deafblind people and Greater Glasgow NHS Board, NHS Lanarkshire, and NHS Tayside began to provide a service. Having a service in medical settings was simply a massive step forward.

In 1998, the final report on the Scottish Office Project confirmed that the guide/communicator service did change the lives of deafblind people; that the role of the guide/communicator is a specialised one and should be recognised as such; and that the service must be fully resourced to be effective.

The Sensing Progress Report was issued in May 1998 by the Scottish Executive, one of several over the next decade. Amongst many other findings it found that "there is no distinct local authority provision for deafblind people". And that "arrangements for assessment and review are at best ad hoc". There was also concern about the ability of smaller authorities to prioritise needs where people were deafblind.

By the late 1990s Margaret Law, who had joined the team some time before as my PA was now heavily involved, along with me in arranging the guide/communicator service which was in great demand. Margaret Law and I were spending most of our time allocating work to the guides and ensuring deafblind people's needs were met. There were many users who we were unable to contact easily, or directly, meaning that if a guide cancelled we couldn't easily let the user know. On a Friday evening we would move mountains to find a replacement, otherwise they might spend most of Saturday waiting for a guide who couldn't come. It was a stressful role and some dedicated people took it on over the years. It was amazingly rewarding when things went well, and soul-destroying when they didn't.

In 1999 at our Usher Syndrome Conference in Abertay University Ove Bejsnap from Denmark spoke about services in Scandinavia. We had been aware for some time that services in Scandinavia were to be envied and Ove explained that in Denmark it is a legal requirement that deafblind people have the services of a Contact Person, for up to 20 hours per week. Ove had brought with him to the conference 2 Contact Persons who provided Hands-on Sign Language support at all times. Remembering this was more than 20 years ago, it was amazing to watch this in action.

We could not aspire to that sort of provision in Scotland, our guides were still being trained in British Sign Language as fast as we could make it happen, the biggest problem being trying to find Deaf tutors. It was also reported that, in Norway, a guide/communicator service is a civil right for deafblind people. Up to 500 hours per year is allowed for each person. In Finland government guidelines state that deafblind people can expect to receive up to 240 hours per year.

The Usher Syndrome Conference noted that Scottish deafblind people were still a long way from their dream of a guide/communicator being available to them in the same way a BSL interpreter is available to a deaf person, free of charge at the point of use. It was said over and over again that, as deaf BSL users who had lost their sight, they felt particularly disadvantaged, indeed discriminated against, by not having the same access to language or communication support. It has to be said that this particular discrimination remains a concern today.

37: "Yes to Access" Campaign, 1999

During 1999/2000 the "Yes to Access" joint campaign involving both Deafblind UK and Sense Scotland attracted the attention of the life peer Jack Ashley who got involved. It also caught the imagination of politicians and the Department of Health, and the press, and within months Section 7 Guidance came into being.

(For detail on this see Chapter 14.) In the meantime, small gains continued.

After almost 3 years of work and preparation, we were heading towards Deafblind Scotland being a separate Scottish charity (see Chapter 13). At the same time the service was growing. In 2001 17,000 hours of guide/communicator service were provided. This was an incredibly busy, stressful time. We were growing a specialist service, establishing a new organisation, campaigning for Section 7 Guidance, and responding to demands for a guide/communicator service.

In 2001 I accompanied Stephen Joyce, our Training Manager, to meet with John Womersley, a consultant in public health medicine, Greater Glasgow NHS Board. Stephen wanted to make him aware of the particular difficulties encountered by people with Usher Syndrome, not only in medical settings but when trying to maintain their health and fitness. This one meeting explained the need very effectively. I was not a qualified interpreter at the time, but as was often the case Stephen had not been able to book an interpreter and I stepped in, which meant I couldn't take part in the meeting. It was, however, yet another example of the benefits of "the great and the good" meeting deafblind people in the flesh. Greater Glasgow NHS Board agreed to fund a limited guide/communicator service to be able to access not only medical appointments but activities designed to improve health and wellbeing.

The effect of this had to be seen to be believed. Wellbeing activities included gym attendance, walking, and swimming. These could now be supported in certain circumstances. More than any other activity we were at that time undertaking this helped to improve the sense of wellbeing within the Deafblind community. Not only did they undertake physical exercise, they often tried to attend the same classes as other deafblind people which meant they could not only exercise, but communicate with others, using tactile means. This was very much encouraged and planned at SAGOD meetings. Even if they could only do this once a week it had a positive effect out of all proportion to the cost of the guide/communicator service provided.

38: Jill McDonald looking at the G/C assignment board in Lenzie office

To illustrate financially how the service was growing in July 2002 I sent a report to Glasgow saying that the service had cost £56,500 in 2001/02. This service had been used by 23 deafblind people. During this period the possibility of increasing the funding available for deafblind people by accessing Transitional Housing Benefit (THB) was raised, for those who didn't have a service. We were advised to pursue this way of funding, where communication needs were tied to housing needs and 11 deafblind people in Glasgow were quickly referred for THB funding with the result that several people obtained a service.

Then funding for the service began very slowly to migrate, one person at a time, to the Community Care budget. We had been funded from the BSL interpreting budget until that time and this change came from left field. Over several years this led to us being funded more and more from Care sources, and to being required eventually to register with Scottish Social Services Council, even although we did not at that time provide care services. This move to care-funded services had major implications which had not been foreseen. We had been for almost 10 years a specialist service. In the end care services finally became chargeable to the individual in a way interpreting, communication and language support did not.

This illustrates one of the problems caused by chasing funding.

We had benefitted from the skills of some very committed service administrators since the service started but it was time to appoint a service-coordinator and in 2005 Suzanne Abatte took on that role, also joining our Senior Management Team which included Allan Clark from Accounts, Margaret Law in the HR role, and me as Chief Executive.

Developing a specialist service

By 2006/7 Deafblind Scotland's service had, over the years, grown to a point where we provided 45,500 hours of guide/communicator service that year to 150 deafblind people across Scotland. Deafblind Scotland had 680 deafblind members in that year. These hours were listed as assignments and arranged and co-ordinated each week using pre-printed cards grouped by user name, date, and time, one for each 3-hour assignment. Around 300 cards were pinned onto a board approximately 4m wide by 1m deep, under the name of the guide/communicator, for each week. Guide/communicators were given their assignments for 2 weeks hence. It seems unimaginable now to run a service like that, but that was how it was done. If a problem occurred the card was turned at right angles to the others until the problem could be solved.

The communication needs of each deafblind service-user were listed on a master list, together with any stated preferences. The jobs were provisionally allocated to guide/communicators, and then moved around as circumstances dictated. Which guide was allocated to each task was decided by the availability of the guide, the communication skills needed, the geographical location, the task to be undertaken, any gender requirements, and any specific requests. This was not an easy service to provide then, and still isn't today. It was stressful for the administrator who was dealing with so many variables and trying to match them. We had several very able, committed co-ordinators over the years. Most guide/communicators worked on a sessional basis, and were limited in the assignments they could fulfil by a variety of factors including the same reasons which affected the allocation of assignments. (e.g. if a deafblind person is going swimming they prefer to go with a swimmer of the same gender, who can also interpret for them).

It took until 2011 to develop an in-house piece of software which worked well enough to meet the need. This did not remove the stress, but it did remove the need for cards and this did help to save the planet.

Creating a profession of caring, trained specialists

Over the previous decade the guide/communicator profession had continued to develop in every way, particularly as regards skills levels. Stephen Joyce, Training Manager, trained hundreds of people in Communication and guiding skills with deafblind people, and in BSL qualifications.

I delivered more than one course on Interpreting (Deafblind Manual) to our guide/communicators. This was a qualification which changed attitudes, and developed professionalism as well as increasing skills levels. Thus I was dismayed when this qualification was withdrawn from Signature's suite of qualifications. Deafblindness is a low-incidence disability and therefore the numbers of guide/communicators required will never be huge. But this group of highly skilled individuals are a key factor in the enabling and supporting of deafblind people. They need a suite of specialist qualifications to aspire to and to work through if standards are to be maintained and improved.

Those who had achieved a suite of communication qualifications at that point went on to undertake the Diploma in Deafblind Studies. At that point the Diploma coordinator had negotiated with Scottish Social Services Council that those holding the Diploma would qualify for Care registration, without having go through the SVQ structure. In the end this offer was not implemented, perhaps due again to the small numbers. But this meant SVQ care modules had to be completed by staff requiring registration and this again meant the reduction of focus on communication skill.

The skills and qualifications of senior guides were well recognised in the world of Language Service Professionals but the inevitable result of the guide/communicator service being under the umbrella of "Care services" was a negative impact on the hourly rate local authorities were prepared to pay. And thus the historical disparity between the hourly rate of the BSL interpreter and the guide/communicator was widened. This obviously impacted on the service's development. The move towards most services, even the specialist ones, being viewed as Care services has marched inexorably on. Deafblind people can feel offended as they do not view a guide/communicator as a carer, but as their equivalent of a BSL interpreter, a highly skilled individual who can meet their communication needs. Indeed, over the years many of the guide/communicators went on to become BSL interpreters.

Fortunately, the guide/communicator role appeals to a wide range of people – people who are interested in others, are interested or qualified in communication skills and want to help those who experience problems with communication, are interested in enabling people, or helping them reach their potential; people who want to open up the world for a uniquely disadvantaged group of people. They need many skills to be a good guide/communicator but one very important skill is to be able to take a back seat and allow and enable the deafblind person to speak for themselves in whatever language or communication mode they use.

However, whatever difficulties then lay in wait for prospective guide/communicators there was no shortage of good people who wanted to pursue this career and it was my privilege to train many of them, watch them develop skills, and watch deafblind people develop skills too as they received the communication support they needed. By this time the original guide/communicators, John, Jim, and Janet had given way to a whole host of guides who found the job uniquely rewarding. Many went on to develop their communication skills to a very high level. Some became BSL interpreters. Up to 70 well-qualified guides across Scotland are now committed to working with deafblind people and available for work, while others are available on an occasional basis as needs demand.

Most of this book is drawn from diaries, articles, and notes, in order to make it as accurate and authentic as possible. I came across an old 2004 note of training participants which showed that J. Donatti, M. Hearns, C. Lawler, G. Lundie, M. Tervitt, B. Welsh, N Styles, L. Lockwood, and J. Knowles were working as guide/communicators in that year, and had been for several years at that time. At the time of writing all of these guides are still working regularly, 17 years later. In addition, mentioned in the same source are J. Lee, R McCourt, C. McGlennon, L. McKenzie, and K. Rhoden, all of whom went on to become BSL Interpreters and are now working with deaf people in the main, but still retain their deafblind skills base.

Chapter 12

"Influencing" - The role of the individual guide/communicator

It seems to me the most useful thing I did in my working life was to work towards creating and developing a guide/communicator service for deafblind people. How that happened – or didn't – is explained in the preceding pages. However, I thought it might help to "meet" 2 guide/communicators and learn about how each one brings something different to the job.

I decided to write about 2 female guide/communicators, both of whom died before their time, while they were working for Deafblind Scotland: Joan Reynolds and Margaret-Anne Duthie. I could have written about any one of dozens of excellent guides over the decades, because there have been many, the vast majority of whom are still alive. But I chose these 2 ladies because they were not going to be embarrassed by the attention given to them. Also, because they were very different from each other, from different backgrounds, they had different interests, different characters, and different abilities. They were both fine examples of people who go the extra mile, strive to keep deafblind people fully informed, put the needs of deafblind people first, and enable them to lead in all situations.

They both served deafblind people in a selfless, dedicated, committed way which was greatly appreciated by deafblind people. And that is the beauty of being a guide/communicator. Each day is different, each deafblind person has a different communication need, different skills set, and each guide/communicator can employ different skills and abilities to meet their needs. Not only their basic communication needs, but their need to accomplish things, to be involved in their communities, and to have some joy in their lives. Sometimes guides find they just can't meet that need, however hard they try, and they have to live with the frustration that can bring.

Joan Reynolds - Guide/communicator Aberdeen

39: Joan Reynolds

Joan Reynolds was an Aberdonian, who lived her life in Aberdeen with her husband Rob and her 2 sons, Paul and Ian. Her family life was all important to her and it was as her boys grew a little that she volunteered with deafblind people. She first met deafblind people in the person of Sabbie Potter when, together with her great friend Isobel Bracewell, they started the Aberdeen Rainbow Club, which allowed deafblind people to get together and enjoy each other's company once a month, in the premises of the Aberdeen and North East Deaf Society.

Sabbie was an inspiration to Isobel and Joan, and to deafblind people in the Rainbow Club: she read Moon books and newspapers, including the sports pages; she delighted to discuss football with her male friends;

she had a phenomenal memory for knitting patterns and could produce an adult sweater every 3 weeks. Even at 84 she was thirsty for new information and experiences and had just recently gone on a mini cruise to Shetland where the locals were fascinated by her Deafblind Manual communication.

At that point Aberdeen Rainbow Club was one of only 3 deafblind clubs in Scotland, the other 2 being in Glasgow, and the volunteers were well aware of its importance. But they were getting older and Isobel, who together with Joan was the mainstay of the club, had MS so it was all becoming a bit more difficult for her. And then the Deaf Club hit financial problems and continued access to the venue became doubtful.

At that time the guide/communicator service was growing in the Central Belt and I was very keen that Aberdeen members had the opportunity to have a similar service. There was new training available for guide/communicators and Joan was persuaded to take a place on it. She had the necessary skills, but not the certificates to prove it. She had a natural instinct to enable people rather than care for them and this was a great start. In the end, she and I became qualified Interpreters in Deafblind Manual on the same course which was arranged by DBUK.

I had watched Joan at work with deafblind people and even before receiving all the communication training she was a natural guide/communicator, always seeking to communicate what people were saying, always taking a back seat, allowing the deafblind person to speak, to represent themselves, to lead, and never speaking for them. But when they weren't given a chance to speak, she would seek permission from the deafblind person, and then intervene politely and firmly to ask for a pause during which the deafblind person could put their point, or otherwise, if they decided not to. She focussed on giving them the information in their chosen communication method and on their understanding of the message given. She would politely ask a speaker to slow down when she couldn't keep up with their pace. She was, simply put, a lady who was full of grace; she walked the walk, and she talked only sparingly.

Over the years she came to meetings in Glasgow even when no Aberdeen members were present. Then she worked as a Deafblind Manual interpreter with whoever needed it. She did it quietly and professionally and was always in demand. In the early days she ensured Aberdeen friends George and Zena, friends who were both deafblind, saw each other once a fortnight. She encouraged them to develop their Deafblind Manual skills for future needs. She visited deafblind people as they were referred to Deafblind Scotland and she met many very lonely individuals across Aberdeen and Aberdeenshire, many of whom were very elderly. And she then visited them as required. Some of them lived in very outlying places and she covered hundreds of miles visiting them. Some of them wrote after her death to say how much her visits meant to them. She viewed deafblind people in hospital as uniquely isolated and ensured, if they had no other visitors, she would visit them.

Several deafblind people over the years asked that Joan be with them when they came to the end of their lives, sometimes in preference to their families. And she never shirked this duty, but faithfully carried out their wishes, often with their families present, communicating with them in Deafblind Manual for as long as she could. One deafblind man said his family had never communicated with him in the way Joan did. One deafblind lady asked that no one come to her funeral except Joan and a DBUK staff member who worked on the Peterborough helpline. Joan had visited her once a fortnight for many years and the helpline lady spoke to her every few days. When she didn't phone the helpline for a week the helpline lady phoned Joan and Joan phoned the relevant people. It was only after her death that Joan discovered the arrangements for her funeral. It is to the organisation's credit that the lady's wishes were met and that both staff members attended.

Joan often displayed one of the classic characteristics of a committed guide/communicator. At meetings, during a break, when lots of people are chatting to other sighted-hearing people, a committed guide/communicator might be found still communicating what's happening around them to the deafblind person.

Joan was a quiet Christian lady who found time for anyone in need. In her spare time she and Rob did voluntary work with the homeless. Unknown to most people, especially deafblind people, she had not enjoyed the best of health for a number of years, and one day took ill suddenly, for a totally unrelated reason, while out doing voluntary work with Rob. She was taken to hospital and later that same day she passed away. The tributes paid to Joan by deafblind people after her death demonstrated their affection for her.

Margaret-Anne Duthie - Guide/communicator Glasgow

40: Margaret-Anne Duthie interpreting for W. Taylor

Margaret-Anne Duthie lived in East Kilbride. She was married to Martin who was the love of her life. He is a keen runner and ran every Saturday, often in races, and Margaret-Anne went to watch him, in hail, rain, or shine. She never took a Saturday off. She loved him more than life itself; he was her best friend and her rock.

She also loved her cats, who ruled her life at home. If the cat miaowed in a particular way she knew it wanted the heating on. Indeed they miaowed constantly if you phoned her. Her old answering machine message used to make Margaret Law, often phoning to help arrange work for guides, chuckle – "please leave the message after the miaow". Goodness knows how she did it but she managed to make that clever cat miaow right on cue.

Margaret-Anne had various jobs when she was younger, working in a golf range, a sports shop, Pizza Hut, and a supermarket. She came to work as a guide/communicator for Deafblind Scotland in 1998. Already having signing skills, she threw herself into learning about being a guide/communicator. She described herself as terrified when she went out on her first solo job. She was fascinated with sign language, a natural signer, who learned more about it by absorbing herself in conversations with deaf people.

She had a huge personality and was interested in everything and everybody. She talked non-stop, and when she wasn't talking she was signing. A lifelong interest in sign language made sure she was a great communicator. If she knew something, could see or hear something, she wanted deafblind people to know about it too. Margaret-Anne could sometimes be challenging to manage and we had some discussions about her role as a guide/communicator. In truth she would do anything for a deafblind person, and was much loved by those whom she worked with. But sometimes she was over-zealous in her efforts to achieve the deafblind person's objectives and might over-promise on what the organisation could achieve.

I fully understood why she occasionally crossed the line. And in truth I loved her for it. She pushed me to achieve more for them. That same dedication to communication meant that I could rest assured that any deafblind people she was working with, knew what exactly was being said to them, knew exactly what their rights were, and exactly what they had to do next. And then she would tell me exactly why she had broken the rules, and exactly what I should do next.

Margaret-Anne was a huge Celtic supporter. She was a major part of the small team which had enabled Clark Steven, who we heard about in Chapter 3, to once more become a football fan, and part of the reason that she could do that was that she was such a fan herself. In Clark Steven's story we tell of the efforts made to find a way to sign a football match in real time. Margaret-Anne's enthusiasm helped convince Clark he didn't need to see the football match; he could feel it. When Celtic reached the UEFA Cup Final in 2003 Clark said he would dearly love to go and we all agreed we just had to try to make that happen.

Margaret-Anne and I contacted everyone we knew to try to find 2 tickets. Between us we made over 100 phone calls, some to people who might be considered slightly dodgy individuals. Then we found a potential ticket, but it could only be picked up in person from a man at Paddy's Market, Glasgow at 6.00am on a dark morning. We agreed the risk was worth the prize, and we also agreed that neither of our husbands should be told about this slightly risky venture. Simply put, Martin might not allow it to happen. We decided that Margaret-Anne would go out on a really early job (to meet the man) and I would be at home live on the mobile the whole time she was there, and I would make sure she could get help if she needed it. Of course, she succeeded. She met a lovely man at Paddy's Market and came away with the required tickets. And a deafblind Celtic supporter's dream could come true, when Christine, the other original member of that small football interpreting team, flew to Porto with him and returned 24 hours later, unfortunately minus the cup.

It is worth noting that many deafblind people go through their lives experiencing depression, or anxiety, or both. Viewed from that perspective the ebullient enthusiasm, the indomitable spirit of a guide/communicator like Margaret-Anne is invaluable.

Margaret-Anne went home from work one evening, sat down in the chair, and when Martin came through to speak to her a few minutes later, she had died, without a murmur, where she sat. She was 44 years old. Her funeral was an out-pouring of emotion and her kind husband, realising the place she held in deafblind people's lives, graciously allowed deafblind people to play their part, ensuring they were given a flower to lay on her coffin, and allowing them to put it into the grave in the same way the family did.

These 2 women held a place in the hearts of deafblind people. They were a little bit special in certain ways, but they were also very typical of the long-term guide/communicators, professionals who are proud when deafblind people achieve things, when they can not only be involved, but take the lead, in any situation, given skilled communication support. Several guide/communicators have been with the organisation since the early days including Margaret, Christine, Gina, Jackie, and many others. Another whole book could be written about the contribution the work of the guide/communicators has made to the lives of the deafblind people.

Chapter 13

"Influencing" - Creating Deafblind Scotland as a Scottish charity

The impact of Scottish devolution

In the mid-1990s in Scotland the move towards devolution was making steady progress. In the summer of 1997, the Scottish Office said that organisations which received funding would need to show that there was real participation by Scottish people in the decision-making process of any organisation. There was a move within Scotland at that time by national organisations and charities to ensure their activities within Scotland were seen to be governed by people within Scotland, and particularly service-users.

The background to the separation of Deafblind Scotland from Deafblind UK

The relationship between the NDBL's head office in Peterborough and their office in Scotland was always a positive one. Ann Barnett, the Chief Executive who had set up the office in Scotland, was committed to the success of the Scottish office and readily agreed to more events being staged in Scotland, as well as there being a Scottish dimension in place for UK events. In Scotland we produced information leaflets using the heading "The League in Scotland" which began to give the Scottish operation its own identity.

This effective working relationship was continued when Jackie Scott became CE. She wrote to me in

1994 agreeing which office could approach which trusts for funding, i.e. "The League will not contact trusts based in Scotland, or those which lean towards Scottish projects for their funding." This meant trust income for the NDBL in Scotland could be increased. By the same token, in Scotland we agreed not to approach English trusts thus maximising income from trusts across the whole organisation. And it has to be said, until the "Field of Dreams" new building came onto the agenda, almost 20 years later, I did not approach English trusts, except on one occasion, and that was with Deafblind UK's agreement.

Organisational name change

In 1996, came the news that the National Deaf-Blind League was to change its name to Deafblind UK. While we in Scotland all agreed this was a simpler name, we were of the opinion that, at this particular time in Scottish history, it would have been helpful to have a name into which it was easy to fit the word Scotland. In November, Jackie Scott issued a memo about terminology saying that "Deafblind UK in Scotland" could be used, but not Deafblind Scotland. I was grateful that Jackie Scott understood that, while we required to remain within legal boundaries, it was beneficial to have a Scottish identity. And 2 years later the name Deafblind Scotland was the name chosen for the new organisation.

A natural progression

Within a year of its inception SAGOD had as a standing agenda item the possibility of setting up a separate charity in Scotland. A charity in which the board of directors would include Scottish deafblind people, finally giving them a real say in the future of deafblind people in Scotland. It took long negotiations, a consultation exercise, and lots of research, to establish the need for a separate Scottish charity, which was finally achieved in 2001. Deafblind people took part in the process with enthusiasm and dedication, serving on the management steering group to set it up, which meant that, finally, when deafblind people became directors of the new charity, they already had essential skills, and could quickly participate in a meaningful way.

At the second meeting of SAGOD, on 5 March 1998, the issue of the Scottish branch of DBUK becoming a separate organisation with its own board of directors had been tabled for discussion, and there was a great deal of enthusiasm for becoming a separate Scottish organisation. I reported that "this had already been informally discussed and a legal separation may become necessary if the Scottish operation continues to grow at the present rate. But the Scottish organisation, in my opinion, should consider remaining part of the national one under a Scottish management committee. That is more or less the model Sense uses."

In 1998 the Scotland Act came into being stating "Scotland will have its own parliament" and it became inevitable that a group which had already been considering its future should consider forming a Scottish charity, in one way or another.

At a SAGOD meeting on 1 March 1999 the 5-year plan was discussed and the formation of a separate Scottish charity became part of that 5-year plan, which, it was understood, Deafblind UK Peterborough would inevitably have to approve or reject.

Jackie Scott, who became Jackie Hicks, had said to me more than once during routine supervision that some of the Deafblind UK directors were ill at ease with the current situation where they had full responsibility for all that happened in Scotland but there was little or no representation on the board from Scotland, and the distance involved meant they weren't able to easily get to know Scottish deafblind people. Jackie felt that becoming a separate Scottish charity was something the board would be willing to explore at some point.

Early in 1999 Jackie sent a memo to me about the proposed development of a 5-year plan for Scotland saying that if we could establish something along the lines of the Sense model, where there remains close contact, then she thought it could work. She added that in order to gain the Board's endorsement of moves to make Scotland a separate entity, they would have to have far more information about the proposed model and the legal processes through which they would have to work.

In June 1999 Lucy Dunbar, having spent some time researching the legal situation, advised me that basically the only option she could see for Scottish deafblind people to have more involvement, more influence, was to become a separate organisation from Peterborough. The Sense model, apparently, retained close ties but did not allow deafblind members to vote. To separate with more involvement and control for deafblind people, we would need to have our own "establishing document", a different name, and our own audited accounts. We would have to become a company limited by guarantee in Scotland. The final stage would be to apply to the Inland Revenue to be considered for charitable status. This was different to the charity registration process in England. I had concerns, as Sense appeared to have a model of devolution which worked, and we were happy to use, but we were no experts and might well be missing something.

At the SAGOD meeting that same month it was agreed that "a proposal should be put to the next meeting of the DBUK Board of Management that there should be a legally separate organisation for Scottish members which remained part of the national organisation. It should be called Deafblind Scotland and the model of devolution used should be the Sense Scotland model." At that point it was still envisaged we could have our own board of directors but remain part of DBUK. There would be reciprocal representation on each board of management.

41: 10th anniversary celebration

The 10th anniversary celebration in September 1999 provided an ideal opportunity for Jackie Hicks, CE

DBUK, Bob Nolan, Chairperson in Scotland, and I to discuss over lunch how we might achieve our aspirations for deafblind people to play a bigger part in the organisation. It was a wonderful opportunity which presented itself at what was a celebration and a social occasion.

Lucy Dunbar, our fundraiser, Margaret Law, PA, and I were charged with guiding NDBL Scotland through the process. We met with Golds Solicitors several times and in October 1999 they wrote to confirm that separation procedures could, in reality, be based on only 2 options in Scotland. We could become a stand-alone organisation, or an organisation which is a subsidiary of DBUK. In the second option deafblind people would not have a vote. In the end the agreement was that Deafblind Scotland should be a stand-alone organisation where Deafblind Scotland would use the logo under licence while we shared common aims. If we truly were to be an organisation led by deafblind people, then their not having a vote was not a realistic option. The aim was that more than 50% of directors were to be deafblind members. This was to be an organisation of, rather than for, deafblind people.

On 9 December 1999 the Management Steering Group was formalised and received training from Lynn Hawcroft. Those involved were John Whitfield, Irene Birse, Michael Anderson, Robert Nolan, Robert Dillon, John Dearie, and me. Over the next 18 months this group sought to take forward the Deafblind UK – Devolution Proposal of July 1999.

I went on a 2-day visit to Peterborough in March 2000 for a series of meetings during which Deafblind UK asked for a business plan, financial information, information on creating the board, staffing structure of the new organisation, and what central services would be required. This information was provided over the following months.

Decision time

Deafblind UK's AGM took place on 18 October at Peterborough United Football Ground. Item 5 on the agenda was the "vote on the resolution to establish Deafblind UK's Scottish office as a separate company".

Dr Gafga, the chairperson, referred to the 5-year corporate plan which had been drawn up by the board and which had made provision to consider the Scottish office in view of the political and financial prevalent situation. He added that the board fully recommended that the resolution be approved. He read out the resolution in full:

> "That the formation by members of Deafblind UK resident in Scotland of a company limited by guarantee and having charitable status as a separate but associated undertaking in order to acquire that part of the assets and undertakings of the charity forming Deafblind UK Scottish office with effect from 1st April 2001 on such terms as may be agreed and consistent with the charity's objects and status be approved and that the directors of the charity be authorised to negotiate and agree the terms of such disposal on behalf of the charity."

Dr Gafga asked for a proposer and seconder and called for a show of hands in favour and a show against. There were none against. Dr Gafga then intimated the result of a postal vote as 165 for and 5 against and therefore announced that the resolution was overwhelmingly approved.

And thus Deafblind Scotland was born, not quite in the format originally foreseen, but in a structure which was acceptable to all. It has to be said that that without Jackie Hicks and Dr Gafga's full support for this measure it would have been much more difficult to make it happen.

Hands around Scotland

42: Hands-around-Scotland group at Aberdeen airport

During the preparation for the new organisation to come into being it was agreed that Deafblind Scotland should start with a bang and a number of suggestions were made – a ceilidh, a party, a convention. In the end it was agreed that every area of Scotland needed to be involved, and one way to do that was to carry a flag from Peterborough to Scotland and then to transport that flag around the whole of Scotland using the most unusual methods of transport we could find.

The relay started when David O'Hare set off from Peterborough early on Wednesday 21 March and travelled to Berwick-upon-Tweed by rail carrying with him the flag of Deafblind Scotland. The next day Michael Anderson travelled to Musselburgh in a fish lorry, and met Desmond Smith who took the flag to Falkirk in a chauffeur-driven car. At Falkirk a vintage Chinese bus was waiting to transport several members to Dunfermline. Charlie Crawford, Margaret Bryce, Elizabeth Burns, Francis Keane, Iris Thomson, Jessica Thomson, Eliza Smith, and Michael Stoddart all took part in their own leg of the journey. On Friday, Margaret Bryce travelled from Dunfermline to Montrose in the front seat of a funeral limousine. At the same time Morag Young made the trip on the back of a Harley-Davidson, while May Fotheringham enjoyed a leisurely trip on a steam traction engine. Irene Birse then took the coastal road to Aberdeen in a 3-wheeled vintage laundry van.

In Aberdeen George Simpson took the flag and boarded a flight to Shetland, meanwhile John Whitfield boarded an oil tanker from Mosmorran to Aberdeen. On Saturday, Bob Nolan travelled from Aberdeen to Inverness with the local mountain rescue team in their land rover, while John Whitfield travelled to John o' Groats. On Monday, Billy Taylor travelled by ferry to Ullapool and then to Stornoway on the Isle of Lewis. Stanley and Shirleyann Harris made the journey from Inverness to Killin on the back of 2 Honda Goldwing motorbikes. They arrived in time to pass on the flag to Michael Stoddart and Billy Don who travelled to Stirling courtesy of the Fire Brigade.

A full week after the journey began, on Wednesday 28 March, Robert Clarke sailed up the Clyde into Glasgow courtesy of the coastguard. And at the same time

Andy McAuley came from Oban in a police car, as a guest. And from Edinburgh, John Dearie and Clark Stevens travelled on the back of Honda Gold Wings to Glasgow. Stephen Joyce came by tandem to the SECC Glasgow and Maria Crawford travelled by vintage sweet van.

The day culminated in a triumphant tour of the city centre by a cavalcade of these vehicles led by an open-top bus full of Deafblind Scotland members. A great deal of publicity was gained from this event – 45 deafblind people had travelled 2000 miles across the length and breadth of Scotland.

43: SECC during Hands around Scotland 2001

Members then gathered in the Marriott Hotel for a celebratory lunch where Jackie Hicks, Bob Nolan, and I addressed the 100-strong group. Following the lunch, the inaugural meeting of the new board of directors took place. The directors appointed were Bob Nolan, John Dearie, Irene Birse, Maria Crawford, John Whitfield, Bill Thomson, Michael Anderson, Bill Crawford, and Michael Stoddart, some of whom had served on the steering group to achieve a new organisation. Bob Nolan was voted as chairperson, Irene Birse as vice-chairperson, and I was appointed as company secretary.

There is no doubt that a great deal of work was involved in bringing about this change. It really was a daunting task. However, it achieved the main objective which was to put deafblind people firmly at the heart of what happens for deafblind people in Scotland.

Deafblind Scotland and Deafblind UK have maintained a good relationship over the years and have worked together where it has best served the needs of deafblind people, a recent example being when Deafblind Scotland sought advice from DBUK on building the new centre in Lenzie. We look forward to continuing cooperation between these sister organisations in the years to come.

Chapter 14

"Influencing" - Section 7 Guidance in England and Wales

Section 7 Guidance was undoubtedly a huge issue for deafblind people and was a major agenda item at SAGOD meetings from 2001 until 2008. Deafblind people genuinely believed that this would come about, that this would happen, in Scotland, in time. There was no logical reason why it wouldn't happen, given that it had brought about improvements in England and Wales, especially if deafblind people used their famous influencing skills. And given that the UK parliament with Section 7 Guidance, and indeed the European Parliament with their Declaration of Rights in 2004, both treated deafblindness as a separate disability.

During 1999/2000 the "Yes to Access" joint campaign involving Deafblind UK, Deafblind UK's Scottish office, Sense UK, and Sense Scotland demanded that deafblind people have a number of hours of communicating and guiding support per week as happened in most Scandinavian countries. The Minister for Disabled People rejected this request but stated that "the government is failing deafblind people" and that he would intervene. During a debate on Jack Ashley's private member's bill, the government announced a widespread consultation looking at deafblind services and the gaps therein. John Hutton from the Department of Health brought together a steering group including Deafblind UK, Sense, RNIB, RNID, Welsh sensory impairment organisations, and social service representatives. He said that if the evidence was compelling that deafblind people should receive special consideration, he would issue the necessary guidance.

The outcome was that, within 6 months, on 9 March 2001 new guidance under Section 7 of the Local Authorities Social Services Act 1970 was issued. Section 7 Guidance stated that local authorities in England and Wales should: identify, make contact with, and record deafblind people in their catchment area; ensure an assessment is carried out by a person specifically trained in deafblindness; ensure that appropriate services are provided to deafblind people, who are not necessarily able to benefit from mainstream services or those services aimed primarily at blind people or deaf people who are able to rely on their other senses; that deafblind people are able to access specifically trained one-to-one support workers for those people they assess as requiring one; should provide information in alternative formats and methods that are accessible to deafblind people; and have a senior member of staff responsible for deafblind services.

It goes without saying that SAGOD initially thought Christmas had come early when Section 7 was introduced in England and Wales. Deafblind people wrote to and lobbied their MSPs and their MPs. Dr Winnie Ewing asked the Executive whether it would issue guidance similar to that issued in England and Wales. Malcolm Chisholm answered that they had no plans to replicate the guidance. Similar questions were asked of ministers over the next 2 years, all from MSPs who had been lobbied by their deafblind constituents.

One reply came from Nicol Stephen who said "a working group would be set up under the Equality Unit to look at recommendations from 'Sensing Progress'." Malcolm Chisholm said that, following a number of seminars, local authorities took up the recommendations contained in the report: "this year the implementation of the recommendations would be checked" and "The executive does not specify a minimum level of qualification for deafblind support workers."

44: Group arriving at Waverley Station, Edinburgh, 2005

It had, in the beginning, seemed inconceivable that similar guidance would not surely follow in Scotland. However, despite Deafblind Scotland and SAGOD's best efforts to have this guidance replicated in Scotland, this did not happen. The Scottish Government felt it could address the issues in other ways, and across the whole range of sensory impairments with no need to recognise the unique nature of deafblindness or its specialisms.

The Scottish Parliament relied on reports "Sensing Progress" (1998), and "Sensory Impairment Action Plan" (2003), as their route to better services for all Scottish people who had a sensory impairment. But the strength of Section 7 had been its focus on deafblindness alone which ensured, for a period of time, that the unique problems associated with that particular group were high on the agenda. These reports tended to assume deafblind people would automatically benefit from improvements to services for deaf people and for blind people, even although, within the sector, it was well known that this assumption was wrong.

45: Margaret Mitchell, Bob Nolan and Drena O'Malley

In 2005 Deafblind Scotland published a report named "Decade of Delay" which reported on the insufficient progress made in providing guide/communicator services in Scotland and the issues remaining to be addressed.

46: Irene Birse lobbying her MSP Andrew Welsh

This was a catalyst for a final campaign to try to achieve Section 7 Guidance in Scotland. John Smith from Hamilton lobbied his MSP, Margaret Mitchell, to garner her support and a proposal was put to the next SAGOD meeting. The result was that, on 4 March 2005, Deafblind Scotland organised a march to the Scottish Parliament when more than 100 deafblind people, guide/communicators and friends marched along the Royal Mile to the Scottish Parliament to hear a debate and meet their MSPs.

The urgent motion Margaret Mitchell, List MSP for Central Region proposed is detailed in John Smith's story in Chapter 3. And you can read more about the march there. But forgive me if we also print it here, it was such an important motion:

> "Deafblindness – That the parliament recognises the European Parliament Declaration of Rights of deafblind people which was formally adopted on 1st April 2004 and recognises deafblindness as a distinct disability separate from hearing or sight impairment; considers that more should be done to identify, correctly assess and provide appropriate services for this unique group who cannot automatically benefit from mainstream services or services for people who are either blind or deaf, and further considers that councils should make appropriate provision for this uniquely disadvantaged group, ensuring that they have the same provision of services as outlined in the guidance issued under section 7 (1) of the Local Authority Social Services Act 1970 for England and Wales."

The gallery was crowded with deafblind people seeking the implementation in Scotland of an equivalent to Section 7 Guidance in England and Wales. Sixty-five MSPs signed the motion. Deputy Minister for Health and Community Care, Rhona Brankin, said she would introduce even stronger guidance in Scotland. And we hoped she would.

Sadly, although the Scottish Parliament and individual MSPs were sympathetic, an equivalent to Section 7 for

Scottish deafblind people did not materialise. Guidance was introduced for Sensory Impairment, covering deaf people, blind people, and deafblind people, and based on the Sensory Impairment Action Plan (SIAP) (2003). Due to its generic nature, it could not fully recognise or deal with the specialisms involved in deafblindness. The plan had developed into one which not only covered all 3 sensory impairments, but was set within the framework of National Outcomes for Community Care, Joint Futures, Single Shared Assessments, and Community Health Partnerships etc. In trying to meet the needs of everyone, while remaining faithful to the various appropriate policy frameworks, inevitably the specialist needs of deafblind people did not take priority in the way they had done in Section 7 Guidance in England and Wales. In the end the tiny island of Deafblindness was lost in an ocean of Sensory Impairment, National Frameworks, Single Shared Assessment, and Joint Futures.

Report on Progress made in England and Wales due to Section 7 Guidance

Michael Anderson and I served on the SIAP steering group and we had made strong representation to the group that they should treat deafblindness as a separate disability and import the recommendations of Section 7 Guidance to Scotland. Following the march to parliament earlier that year, the SIAP group asked what the outcome had been following implementation in England, so we undertook to carry out the research into just this question. This involved collating information from Sense surveys 2002–2005, Deafblind UK reports, and the responses to a

Deafblind Scotland Questionnaire sent to councils in England.

The responses received showed that more than 80% of councils responding had identified hitherto unknown deafblind people as a result of Section 7 implementation. The number of deafblind people known to councils had increased by a staggering 67% over 2 years. We identified 29 councils as having specialist workers with the word "deafblind" in their title, and a further 23 had formal arrangements with Sense or Deafblind UK to carry out assessments on their behalf. Of 163 councils taking part in the survey, 101 had seen an increase in the number of hours of guide/communicator service provided and 46 councils were providing a service on request. 30% more people were enjoying the benefits of a guide/communicator service and almost all of the councils had appointed a senior manager responsible for deafblind services.

There had been an obvious and substantial effort since 2001 to train staff in deafblind awareness with a total of 1722 staff across 163 councils having undergone certificated training in deafblindness, and 588 staff having since undertaken further certificated training. This would have contributed greatly to an increasing awareness of deafblindness. When we asked the responsible managers what the impact of Section 7 Guidance had been there was unanimous agreement that, while much remained to be done, the impact of Section 7 Guidance had been both positive and substantial. It had caused minds to focus on deafblindness and this in itself had brought about improvement and greater awareness.

Transitional Housing Benefit (THB)

The situation for deafblind people, in terms of accessing a guide/communicator service was temporarily improved when, under Supporting People, Transitional Housing Benefit became available for some deafblind people to get help with "maintaining their tenancy" e.g. reading mail, completing forms, fixing repairs, paying the rent etc. There were 21 activities considered to be housing support tasks. Social workers, with good intentions, worked to categorise some of the guide/communicator hours they needed as Housing Support in order to gain deafblind people more communication support. And a number of deafblind people did gain a service, which was greatly welcomed.

However, it was around that time that I began to feel a sense of unease about the arrangements being put in place for deafblind people, which were concerned with their tenancy rather than their language, communication, and guiding needs. Unlike Deaf people whose first language was BSL they had no "right" to interpreting or communication support, which was free at the point of access for Deaf people. Some were being given communication support to achieve an aim which others had deemed important. However worthy the aim was, it was not access to interpreting/communication support in the way BSL users enjoyed, and had previously been enjoyed by deafblind people too, when they were viewed as deaf only, and, indeed, when their service was funded by Sign Language Interpreting services. Later there were other versions of funding, all attached to a purpose.

Then Self-Directed Support (SDS) began to be introduced, offering some promise in terms of activities which could be pursued, but at that point, unlike THB, these hours required a client contribution which inevitably means the user can do less with the support. And it re-enforced the link between deafblind people's needs and Care. SDS is and was in that mould of communication support for "worthy aims" which others assess as necessary and therefore may well fund.

The hourly rate local authorities were prepared to pay for support, including for a skilled guide/communicator with a range of communication skills, came under more and more pressure. BSL interpreters earned £30–£40 per hour. Well-qualified guide/communicators were paid £13 per hour. Once the rate paid by local authorities became associated with "care" which is equated with lower pay, the guide/communicator service struggled to fund the level of training required to create specialist workers. The training previously provided had done a lot to make being a guide/communicator an attractive career path. The provision of Signature Level 1, 2, and 3 courses which could lead to a place in the Diploma in Deafblindness was a real incentive to those interested in the field of deafblindness and in communication and linguistic access. The hourly rate paid by local authorities at that point threatened the continuance of this specialist training.

The guide/communicator service had made great strides since it started in 1995, increasing in size, and in quality, and in the skills level of its workforce. There have been times of uncertainty since then, however, it remains a progressive service. But without the driving force of specific guidance on deafblindness most deafblind people have had to fight as individuals for a service, and some over a sustained period, which is discouraging for them. However, that in no way detracts from the tireless work done by deafblind people to achieve a guide/communicator service for those who need it. And there is the hope and expectation that the recognition given to deafblindness and to Tactile BSL within the BSL (Scotland) Act 2015 will, over time, lead to better things for deafblind people.

Chapter 15

"Influencing" - BSL (Scotland) Act 2015

Amongst Scottish Deaf people there was a long-held dream that BSL could be recognised in legislation not only in linguistic terms but as a language whose worth should be recognised and promoted. As a Sign Language Interpreter, and long-term supporter of Deaf people I was delighted by the prospect of having legislation. As a Deafblind Manual Interpreter and supporter of deafblind people I wondered if it might just be possible to include some of the rights and needs of deafblind people in any legislation.

The first time British Sign Language featured strongly in a session of the Scottish Parliament was on 16 February 2000 when Cathie Craigie MSP and Winnie Ewing MSP tabled a motion for debate on BSL. The Presiding Officer, David Steel, agreed BSL should be looked at in greater detail. The year 2000 saw the small, apparently insignificant, steps taken which would assist with the development of the BSL (Scotland) Bill and to an Act of Parliament finally being passed 15 years later. The BSL and Linguistic Access working group was set up by the Scottish Parliament in November 2000 with Lilian Lawson as chairperson. Whenever possible I attended meetings and facilitated deafblind people's involvement. But even when I couldn't be there, I knew Lilian Lawson would mention and advocate for the needs of deafblind people whenever she could. Over the years she, and the Scottish Council on Deafness (SCoD), proved to be invaluable supporters of deafblind people. Likewise, if

I were at a meeting where there was no deaf representation, I would suggest what the needs of deaf people might be.

In February 2005 I presented a paper at the Cross-Party Group on Deafness "Creating Linguistic Access for Deaf and Deafblind People – A Strategy for Scotland" which stated that:

> "the difficulties deafblind people face in achieving linguistic access are recognised as:
>
> Lack of recognition of the need to make special arrangements if deafblind people are to be included, and if they are to have access to information. language, communication, and to the environment
>
> Lack of funding to provide the necessary communication and guiding support services
>
> Lack of skilled Language Service Professionals to provide the support."

The appeal of the group for me was that it was based on linguistic access whatever that might involve, with BSL being the priority need. The group itself represented all who had linguistic access needs and represented a wide range of communication methods within its membership. But the points listed above were those which SAGOD wanted to be addressed. Perhaps the hoped-for BSL Bill could also meet some of the needs deafblind people have. The field of deafness had always been at the back of the queue and this had been the case for many years. So, progress was slow and included a Review of Audiology.

Cathie Craigie, in the end, tabled a private member's bill in 2010, the aim of which was to establish BSL as an official language in Scotland, which could then be taught in schools. However, this attempt failed when, in the Scottish Parliament election, Cathie lost her seat. Undaunted, Cathie encouraged Mark Griffin MSP to take up the mantle, after he was elected as List MSP representing the Central Region.

Mark was already well aware of the difficulties deaf people faced as his grandparents had been deaf, so he truly hit the ground running. Mark began working with the Deaf organisations and with the Scottish Parliament Non-Governmental Bill Unit to get together a bill which would work, and be acceptable to the Scottish Parliament. A consultation took place which encouraged even more responses than Cathie Craigie's – 222 written responses and a petition with 937 signatures.

On 29 October 2014, Mark lodged the proposal for the bill. Now things were really under way, it really was time to find a way in which the needs of deafblind people could be included, as I was so aware if deafblindness wasn't specifically included then this Bill would simply pass deafblind people by and they would not benefit. I didn't envisage the Bill bringing life-changing benefits for deafblind people, but not to be specifically included would be the final straw for deafblind people, after failing to get Section 7 implemented. And, more worryingly, the benefits from BSL being recognised as a language might have been seen by many to automatically meet any needs deafblind people had and this was simply not the case.

So we embarked on a campaign to have "Tactile BSL" included in the Act.

Deafblind people were not mentioned in any of the original papers or the draft bill, however, the Scottish Council on Deafness News issue 33 of 2015/16 contains the quote "'the challenge for me was to ensure that Deafblind BSL users were included in the Bill.' D. O'Malley." So I had been frank since the beginning that deafblind people wanted their needs to be included.

On 30 January 2015, Mark came along to speak to a SAGOD meeting in Glasgow at which Scottish Government's Angela Bonomy spoke about the See Hear Report and Heather Palmer spoke about SDS. Deafblind people were there in some numbers, as usual, using a whole range of communication methods, only one of which was BSL. As is often the case, they were being given an opportunity to have their comments on the BSL Bill filmed while communication support was available at SAGOD.

Mark was able to meet with some of them and learn about the difficulties deafblind people face in getting communication support and how much it meant to them to have deafblindness and Tactile BSL recognised. He agreed to meet with us to discuss ways Tactile BSL could possibly be included.

And that was the start of finding a way to ensure Tactile BSL was named in the Act. A number of ways were discussed as to how to do it and, in April, Ruth Dorman and I met with Mark Griffin MSP and Hilary Third (Scottish Government Equality Unit) at the Scottish Parliament when we all agreed the phrase to be used was "Tactile BSL". While we wanted this included, we did not want to impede the Bill's progress in any way, as deafblind people were never intended as the main beneficiaries. Now it remained to convince Deaf people, MSPs, and Ministers that this move was essential. Stephen Joyce and I met with Stewart Maxwell, Committee Convenor, and I met with Dr Alasdair Allan, minister for Scotland's languages, with deafblind men Frank Thomson and Robert Dillon. The committee listened to their stories. The Deaf community understood.

Throughout May, deafblind people who used Tactile BSL lobbied their MSPs, including R. Dillon who lobbied Stewart Maxwell, S. Joyce lobbied Siobhan McMahon, F. Thomson lobbied Colin Beattie, and A. Muir and A. Dobbie lobbied Mark Griffin. Most MSPs had never met a deafblind person, and it was a steep learning curve for them.

47: Stephen Joyce, Robert Dillon, Ken Halsworth, Willie Dixon, Drena O'Malley and Desmond Smith in the Parliament cafe

On 2 June 2015 an amendment was moved in Parliament by Dennis Robertson: "Both the visual and tactile form of BSL to be included in the Bill." This was passed. Deafblind men D. Smith, R. Dillon, S. Joyce, and I spoke to Stewart Maxwell, Mark Griffin, and

Dennis Robertson who is registered blind, to thank them for their support during the entire process.

The Stage 3 final debate and vote on the British Sign Language (Scotland) Bill finally took place on 17 September 2015. Many deafblind people were up in the balcony, nervously accessing the debate in whatever method they normally use, most using Tactile BSL. There were interpreters everywhere, not only on the floor of the house, but on the balcony working with deaf people, or deafblind people who could still see signing at a particular distance. The excitement in the air was palpable; the importance of the moment was not lost on anyone who was there. In the end, the Bill was unanimously, and almost ceremonially, passed into law, with no further amendments made, and became the British Sign Language (Scotland) Act. There were tears, and a standing ovation Deaf-style, with people waving their arms in the air. At the end Mark Griffin MSP said it was

> "a fantastic example of a minority group in our society coming together, forming a cross party group and lobbying members..."

Rightly there were celebrations, and huge smiles. I still get a lump in my throat when I think of being in the balcony of the Scottish Parliament that day, as deafblind people shed tears when they realised the Bill had just been passed.

48: Mark Griffin MSP with Stephen Joyce celebrating the vote on the BSL Bill

At the time of writing, however, there remains a concern for deafblind people who use Tactile BSL. They continue to suffer the ignominy of being considered to be in need, not of linguistic access, but of care. And due to their linguistic access support being funded from the Social Care budget, they are the only group of people in Scotland who have to pay for linguistic access. The vast majority of deafblind people do not receive care in the normal sense of the word, but support with language and also with guiding. Yet they must undergo a lengthy financial assessment, after which most then have to contribute to the cost of that language support. Surely this is an unintended discrimination which should end. This enigma will hopefully be addressed within the National and Local Plans.

Conclusion

49: Drena O'Malley with Hilary Third from the Equality Unit

The history of the effort put in by deafblind people and staff at Deafblind Scotland is recounted in this chapter for the purpose of encouraging deafblind people and others that, although they are a small group of people talking about a little-known disability, when they are "out there" with their skilled communication, resilience, and adaptability, fully on show, can bring about change. They just need a little understanding from those in power. And during the BSL lobby, they got just that.

Chapter 16

Projects which impacted on the lives of deafblind people

Over a period of 20 years, projects funded by the Scottish Government, Big Lottery Fund, Trusts, and others, played an important part in the development of both deafblind people themselves, and the services available to them. It seems appropriate to me that projects enjoy a place in history. A few have been chosen in this chapter to illustrate the major part projects can play in an organisation, in the development of services, and most importantly in the quality of life of a uniquely disabled group of people. From small acorns…

Deafblind people in Scotland were offered unique opportunities to experience an improved quality of life through the organisation receiving project funding to achieve specific aims. I have written about some of the bigger ones, and some which were simply much loved by deafblind people. Deafblind Scotland was sometimes described as an organisation which "punched above its weight", and part of the reason for this was undoubtedly due to project funding to enable deafblind people to represent themselves.

Guide/communicator service

Much has been written about the guide/communicator service in this book and I won't repeat it here. But it is worth pointing out that the first, and probably the most important, project funding we received was the £5000 project funding received from Strathclyde Regional Council in 1994/5 to train potential guide/communicators and pilot a small guide/communicator scheme. It was a small sum of money but enabled a significant step to be taken on a long journey.

This project also helped secure Section 10 funding from the Scottish Office Home and Health Department 1995–98 for a longer project to develop a service across Scotland. The support for a guide/communicator service given by Strathclyde Regional Council demonstrated by the funding helped to make many authorities aware of the importance of a guide/communicator service to a deafblind person and several small services began as a result of it. The need for a guide/communicator service finally began to be recognised, all made possible initially by a grant of £5000.

The vital training of potential guide/communicators in the first decade was also project-funded by Scottish Office Social Work Services Inspectorate, and by the following trusts: RS Macdonald, MacRobert, Robertson, Garfield Weston, Lintel, and Nancy Massey. This funding allowed the organisation to provide good-quality services delivered by a small but growing number of well-trained professionals.

Usher Syndrome Project

In 1996 the National Lottery Charity Board, following long discussions about the specialist needs of people with Usher Syndrome, granted £277,000 over 3 years to identify people with Usher Syndrome, and to increase their access to services. Stephen Joyce, who himself has Usher Syndrome, was employed as Project

Coordinator and travelled the length and breadth of Scotland meeting people with Usher Syndrome some of whom had never met anyone else who had Usher Syndrome. They had had little contact with any kind of services before meeting Stephen. Bob Nolan, our chairperson from 2001 until 2019, was identified by this project when Stephen met him at an Usher Awareness session in Aberdeen.

Scottish Advisory Group on Deafblindness (SAGOD)

The story of SAGOD is told in a separate section, such is the importance of SAGOD to the story of deafblindness in Scotland. The group had been set up to influence policy at an organisational, local, and national level, but operated only in Glasgow area. Vital funding from Comic Relief over 3 years from 2000 enabled this group to meet and campaign across the whole of Scotland. This project did much to create a group of people who could take forward to politicians and statutory authorities, the needs of deafblind people and how these might be met. They were a force to be reckoned with. One social worker from Aberdeen said at a SAGOD meeting in Angus "I've never been involved in such an effective consultation meeting. I couldn't stop them talking. It was wonderful. Whatever you are doing, keep doing it." And as we saw in Chapter 13, in the end, SAGOD took forward to DBUK the proposal that there might be a separate Deafblind Scotland.

Primetime

An outstanding project which deafblind people loved and still talk about was the Primetime project 2008–11. This was a competition run by the BBC and the Big Lottery Fund with 6 organisations chosen to make a film about their projects which would appear on television, with the winner being the organisation receiving the most public votes. Deafblind Scotland was lucky enough to succeed and to receive £395,525 in funding over the 3 years. The project's aim was to create awareness of deafblindness and Deafblind Manual by teaching children, clubs, Social Work departments, and organisations how to use Deafblind Manual. All awareness teaching was to be undertaken by deafblind people themselves, who were specially trained to deliver this training. John Whitfield was project manager. Over the life of the project 7000 schoolchildren became aware of Deafblind Manual and how to use it, as did 1000 adults. And deafblind people were trained to represent themselves in various situations.

This project created a resource, a pool of specially trained deafblind people, who grew in confidence as they learned new skills. The deafblind volunteers just loved going into schools and teaching the children, and if I could recreate one project from my years at Deafblind Scotland it would be this one. The direct benefit to deafblind people was palpable. In an ideal world deafblind people should be continuing their voluntary work in schools, but the guide/communicator hours embedded in that project, 2600 of them each year of the project, made a tremendous difference, enabling all who wanted to participate to do so, whether or not they had a local authority-funded service of their own.

Numeracy and literacy

Another series of small projects which brought huge benefits to deafblind people were the Numeracy and Literacy projects, which took place over the years 2004 to 2010. The largest was funded by Glasgow City Council but other local authorities were involved too. Glasgow's representative met some deafblind people in Deafblind Scotland's office in Lenzie and very quickly realised that this group of people had even greater problems than those for whom English is a second language.

Therefore, over a period of several years we received funding to employ part-time literacy tutors who worked 1:1 with deafblind people to improve their literacy, and sometimes numeracy skills. With the principles of the English language being skilfully interpreted to deafblind sign language users, many for the first time, we could often see the penny drop regarding how to complain, or how to ask for help, or how to negotiate in written English.

Deafblind people wrote their stories, and improved their English in doing so; one man brought along a boxful of BB medals and badges he had gained, and slowly catalogued them with the tutor's help. Another brought his football programmes over weeks and catalogued them. He learned them off by heart, in order, and could that way show them to others. It was a very sad day when funding for this project finished.

Identification projects

As a result of the introduction of Section 7 Guidance in England and Wales, which required local authorities to identify their deafblind population, a number of Scottish local authorities decided to follow this guidance, believing it would soon be implemented in Scotland. One requirement of Section 7 Guidance was that local authorities should identify and make contact with deafblind people in their area. Therefore in 2002–03 a series of Identification projects was funded by different local authorities in an attempt to get ahead of the game.

Over a year Identification projects were undertaken across Scotland. Using a standard methodology, we were able to help local authorities to identify the deafblind people living in their area. Local meetings were arranged, the projects were widely publicised, Social Work and Health services spoke to those they were in contact with. Services for blind people and for deaf people played an important role in identifying those who may have the second sensory loss. Over the year, in Edinburgh 57 deafblind people were identified, North Lanarkshire 45, South Lanarkshire 61, in Aberdeen 52, in Aberdeenshire 65, and in East Dunbartonshire 24. All of them were put in touch with services and with other deafblind people. It was a simple demonstration of how many deafblind people who fit the European definition are out there – if we but look for them. Sadly Section 7 Guidance never made it to Scotland, but even the possibility of it happening brought about this very useful project.

Health projects

In 2002 a 3-year Joint Healthy Living Project including both Sense Scotland and Deafblind Scotland was funded by the Big Lottery Fund. The aim was to create an understanding of health, diet, the benefits of exercise, and how to improve mental health. Seventeen new posts were created from a grant of £902,000, one of the largest grants Deafblind Scotland ever received. The project covered both congenital and acquired deafblindness across the whole of Scotland and hundreds of deafblind people directly benefitted.

Three years later, in 2005, a 3-year health project was funded to improve the wellbeing of deafblind people by encouraging and enabling deafblind people to use mainstream activities like fitness classes, gyms, running clubs etc. Peter Lavelle led a team to do this. Funding also covered training for mainstream providers to make their services more accessible to deafblind people. Many clubs and leisure centres took a real interest in making their services accessible to local deafblind people. One outstanding example was a boxing club local to Deafblind Scotland's office which undertook to enable a deafblind man, who had previously been a boxer, to train in the gym with the local boxers. At the time of writing James Peline is still involved with his trainer Tam, and the club, who are very proud of his commitment.

Deafblind people can volunteer too

An important example of project funding is the 3-year Social Development Project 2008–11 to encourage social interaction, the development of confidence, communication skills, and retail skills, through the establishment of a retail charity outlet staffed by deafblind people and their guide/communicators. The Moffat Trust, Agnes Hunter Trusts, SBAAT, Gannochy Trust, Lloyds Foundation, and the Hugh Fraser Foundation together contributed £76,000 to enable this to happen.

Welfare Rights project

In 2014 we achieved funding from the Big Lottery Support and Connect Fund, having previously failed twice to achieve funding from this source. This project was aimed at Deafblind, Deaf, and Blind people, all 3 groups. The funding was greatly welcomed when it was finally achieved. The aim was to enable blind and deafblind people to experience less financial hardship, to maximise their income by receiving one-to-one advice on welfare benefits, and to be more informed about decision-making processes which affect their lives. This project, led by Helen Campbell, has continued with other funding from various sources, until the time of writing. This is critically important ongoing work which now offers support and advice to 350 sensory-impaired people annually. It has enabled hundreds of deaf, blind, and deafblind people to access benefits they did not even know about. Total monetary benefit achieved since 2014 now totals over £2.5 million. This includes additional benefits gained, increases in existing benefits, grants for equipment, and blind person's tax allowance etc. This does not include gains which cannot be quantified in monetary terms, e.g. blue badge applications, housing applications etc. Once the benefit is gained by the individual it is often ongoing. Being able to provide a home visit to help complete the application form provides continuity and builds confidence in the sensory-impaired person.

BSL (Scotland) Act 2015

In 2015, 2 years' funding was granted by the Scottish Government Equalities Unit to enable BSL-using deafblind people to input to the development of BSL plans by supporting their attendance at some National Advisory Group (NAG) meetings. To enable deafblind people to attend high-level, formal, official meetings involving large numbers of people is a challenge of epic proportions and this funding was critical to doing that. Hands-on Signers require assistance at all times. There is no downtime. Two hands-on interpreters and one hands-on guide/communicator were on duty at every meeting. Debra Wherrett and Leona Glennie attended almost every meeting. Deafblind people had preparation meetings on top of that, and Ken Hallsworth from Deafblind Scotland and Derek Todd from Deaf Scotland worked together to try to provide both appropriate venues and appropriately qualified interpreters and guide/communicators to service the need.

This was a very difficult task, performed willingly by people who were committed to genuine involvement of the user group. This was part of funding distributed to deaf organisations to ensure they could help with the production of plans which fully involved deaf people.

It is worth noting here that finding appropriate venues to hold a meeting for deafblind people proved to be a challenge of epic proportions. Unfortunately,

Deafblind Scotland's new building was not yet opened, or it may have solved the problem of a venue for NAG meetings.

Conclusion

The projects I have listed above are only a few of the major projects which have taken place at Deafblind Scotland, and it is far from being a complete list, there are many others, often smaller ones. The impact of all these projects has been immense, and cannot be underestimated. The impact on the quality of life of deafblind people has been uniquely positive. Without the funding that enabled them to happen, vital advances for deafblind people would not have taken place. The challenge is to retain the benefits they have brought about for deafblind people once funding is finished. In recent times the most impactful project for individuals has been the Welfare Rights service, which has brought about so many benefits for individual deaf, blind, and deafblind people. This is an essential service. It is inconceivable that in future this service may not be available. But this is always the risk with project-funded services.

Chapter 17

The journey to buying the land

A new challenge

The need for deafblind people to have a safe and easy to access venue which provided accommodation appropriate to their needs had long been recognised. A place where they were able to function independently, communicate easily with others, pursue learning of all kinds, attend meetings in surroundings which maximise communication rather than minimise it, and socialise with others. This chapter tells the story of how the decision was made to build a new centre, and the part deafblind people played in making it happen.

The need for appropriate accommodation

In the early days when The League was based at Barrowfield Deaf-blind Complex. The lounge was often made available to NDBL Scottish office for meetings and we were incredibly grateful for this, but it had endemic problems, the main one being it was a lounge for relaxing in the evenings, full of furniture and not easy to access for a deafblind person.

We also appreciated having the use of St Vincent's Centre for the Deaf in Tobago Street, Glasgow, now no longer there. This was great, but the wooden floor created problems with noise. And we used Visibility Scotland's accommodation at St George's Cross for a social club on a Monday evening. RNID allowed us the use of their office for a monthly Doers' meeting. All were graciously given for our use, but they were far from ideal for use by people with a dual sensory loss.

Over the years staff spent many hours searching for venues for meetings, conferences, and social outings which would be suitable and even enabling for deafblind people. Very few existed. We found newer hotels were often bright and shiny which creates unhelpful glare. They were often neutrally decorated which means the décor can lack the contrast needed to easily find the door. They normally had hard floors, few soft furnishings, and therefore lots of echo. For a hearing-aid user, noise reverberated from, not only the floor, but from every surface. Older hotels and other buildings were often dark, poorly lit places.

Most accommodation we could borrow or rent could not be expected to take into account the needs of those who have a dual sensory loss. Deafblind people need controllable lighting, both artificial lighting and sunshine. A sad sight at a meeting on a bright day might be several deafblind people who have Retinitis Pigmentosa wearing baseball caps **and** with their hand up to further shield their eyes. And most deafblind people need good sound equipment, with a working loop system.

Michael Anderson said of venues

> "Almost without exception, venues required considerable adaptation, and preparation by DbS staff, in particular the setting up of loop systems for the benefit of hearing-aid users, before a meeting could take place. This often required laying a cable round the room and taping it down, on hands and knees.

Fortunately a loop system is now a legal requirement in public venues, but they can still be problematic. In terms of lighting it was rarely adaptable enough to make it work well for most people."

While researching for this book I came across some old supervision notes and the most common negative comment was about the limits imposed on staff by working in overcrowded accommodation in separate venues.

The building blocks of accommodation

50: Office premises at 21,23,27 Alexandra Ave

51: Two flats one up, at 23 Alexandra Ave

The accommodation story really began in 1993 when Ann Barnett, then Chief Executive of NDBL, agreed that we could look for new accommodation and leave Barrowfield. Ann came up to view 4 offices in the Glasgow area and chose Lenzie due to its proximity to the railway station which had great connections to both Glasgow and Edinburgh.

A series of tenement properties in Lenzie, beginning with 21 Alexandra Avenue in 1994, were bought as an office, training centre, rehab flat. The final acquisition was a second flat at number 23 in 2004 bought for training purposes. The total spent was £209,000.

Apart from the final purchase of the flat in 2004, all of these purchases were initially funded by head office in Peterborough on the understanding that the Scottish office would fundraise for these amounts as and when possible. This could only happen due to an important decision taken in 1990 when it was agreed by Ann Barnett that funds we raised in Scotland would be spent in Scotland, while my salary would be paid by NDBL.

The purchase price for the potential training centre at 25/27 felt like, and was, a huge sum of money to raise. Several Scottish trusts supported our efforts to increase the facilities available to deafblind people. This small space really was the hub for them. Just 8 metres by 4 metres the training room really was a revelation. It was carpeted, so was quiet, had blinds and curtains to cut out glare, good contrasting colours, a tea-making facility, and it was theirs. It also served as a training facility to learn BSL, a small place where communication could thrive.

Looking back, our purchase of accommodation might have been described as "lego-like". Deafblind Scotland had been created in 2001 and the final property was directly purchased by the new Scottish charity. It was agreed this purchase would allow reserves in the form of property to be developed. The eventual sale of property in 2016/17 played an important role in funding "Field of Dreams". Not only that, but over the period, Deafblind Scotland's accommodation costs were reduced due to paying limited amounts in rent. Longer term, the property strategy proved beneficial to the charity.

The decision-making process

After the establishment of a separate Scottish charity in 2001, a second 5-year plan 2005–10 was developed with deafblind people and made public. Having appropriate accommodation was an obvious objective to aim for:

> "Develop accommodation in a suitable location, which can provide appropriate surroundings where deafblind people can learn, develop skills and interact with others, and in which staff can function effectively."

This aim became a standing agenda item which would not go away.

It was recognised that we continued to outgrow our accommodation. Having rented additional office space at 25 Townhead in Kirkintilloch in 2000, and purchased an additional flat in Lenzie in 2004, there remained a constant need for more accommodation, both for office staff and in particular for deafblind people to use for activities.

This was due in part to our success in achieving project funding. The Usher Syndrome Project, the Healthy Living Centre Project, the Numeracy and Literacy Project, 2 Scottish Office-funded projects, and Primetime, to name but a few. These projects meant new staff were appointed. There were now 20 staff employed, 45 sessional guide/communicators, and 7 project staff all of whom needed access to accommodation. Project staff were accommodated at 25 Townhead but staff were still using the Training Centre in Lenzie more than deafblind people were, and we were crammed in like sardines. As we grew as an organisation, the accommodation problems also grew.

In 2005, an Accommodation Sub-group was set up to look at alternatives in accommodation. Members of this group were Michael Anderson, Irene Birse, Bill Brown, Bill Thomson, Alistair McLellan, and me. The group would research the options available and report to the Board.

The Accommodation Sub-group

At the first meeting it was agreed that, in principle, any new premises should ideally be approximately 7000–10,000 square feet in size with a large meeting room, close to a railway station, located in Central Scotland or to the north of Glasgow, near a motorway, with parking, and that premises should be easy to travel to from all over Scotland.

Now a picture had begun to emerge of what was needed. And so the journey to new accommodation began. As the years went by the name of this group would change several times in the end becoming the New Build Group. Their priorities would change. The membership would change with Michael Anderson and I remaining involved throughout. In the end the group would be meeting frequently and also prior to every board meeting.

During 2006 the group undertook a programme of visiting premises to gain an idea of what might be available to renovate and convert to new premises for Deafblind Scotland. This idea of renovation was revisited several times. None was found which was appropriate for conversion to meet the needs of deafblind people. New charity premises visited included the new Spina Bifida Hydrocephalus Scotland building in Dullatur, a purpose-built building designed to meet their needs. The Accommodation Sub-group were impressed by the new building in Dullatur, and the idea of trying for a new build was first mentioned. But the first problem with that idea was that we would need land to build on.

The Kirkintilloch's Initiative site

52: Aerial photograph of the "Field of Dreams" site

53: First Site visit

In April 2007 I wrote to Colin Smith of HG Consulting, the Project Manager for Kirkintilloch's Initiative (KI) saying that I had heard that "a charity has obtained a piece of land next to the new road" and adding "I am hoping against hope that there may be another piece of land, as yet unknown to me, which may need a new owner".

Then by chance one Friday night I met Colin, whom I knew on a personal basis, in the local supermarket. After exchanging pleasantries Colin asked if Deafblind Scotland was still interested in buying a piece of land, as one might now become available. To which I replied we would be very interested... and thus – although we didn't quite know it at the time – the story of "The Field of Dreams" began.

In early November 2007 Colin contacted me to say the piece of land we had discussed could now become available as it looked as if the charity currently interested in the land at Lenzie might have to withdraw. Without hesitation, and without a brass farthing in a building fund, I said of course Deafblind Scotland would be interested.

A brainstorming meeting where the land would be discussed was due to take place on 14 November 2007 and Colin phoned me to invite me to the meeting. All the movers and shakers were there and the difficulties were discussed. In the end it was agreed another buyer would now be sought and Deafblind Scotland could potentially become involved in that process.

That same month it was agreed that I would pursue possibilities to purchase that piece of land until there was a good reason to stop.

Such a lot was at stake that, as an organisation, we agreed to regularly review, and to take stock to make sure our journey continued to be a safe and sensible one. Several times over the period we revisited the opportunity to rent property and renovate to suit our needs. At that point it was found that rental costs could be £64,000 plus per year for large enough accommodation. This could be a major addition to core costs which was not an attractive prospect.

We were also hostage to fortune when things happened which were outwith our control, including potential partners in purchasing the land decided it was not for them; the size of the useable land being reduced; the plot being added to SEPA's flood plain. However, East Dunbartonshire Council and Kirkintilloch's Initiative needed us to commit or otherwise by a deadline, and it was agreed to enter into negotiations to purchase the whole site – if necessary – for a cost not exceeding £375,000. In December 2007 we made that commitment, by the deadline, and the journey began.

The journey to Agreement to Purchase

Over the next 2 years while purchase discussions were ongoing there were periods when we were overcome by doubts and concerns. My instruction remained that I should continue to pursue possibilities until there was a good reason to stop.

The driving force for me was that, in the meantime, the problems with accommodation continued to grow. There was now no space which deafblind people could use at will, as it was being used for training purposes. Staff were short of space, privacy, and facilities.

Now we had agreement, in principle, to purchase we could begin to fundraise. It was a great encouragement when Bob and Louise Nolan undertook the LEJOG tandem ride in 2008 raising more than £34,000 for "Field of Dreams", much of it from their many friends across England, some of whom they visited on the way. The tenacity to cycle 100 miles per day for 14 days, and to arrive in time for fundraising events in the evening has to be seen to be understood. My husband, Hammy, and I were the support team for that ride, and others, and it was so encouraging to see the support received from the general public along the way. They would sometimes track us down to give us a donation.

Long and intensive negotiations took place during 2008/09 to reduce the price to be paid for the land, as times had changed, the recession had undoubtedly reduced its value, the size of the plot was slightly reduced now that the road was complete, and the noise-reducing bunds along the road length had also reduced the amount of land available for building. It was considered the cost now should realistically be around £220,000 and this would be the maximum figured offered.

On 26 October 2009 Deafblind Scotland made an offer of £200,000 for the land and this was accepted at an extraordinary meeting of Kirkintilloch's Initiative, payment to be made in November 2010. Planning permission had to be in place before the purchase price was paid. We finally had an agreement to purchase, with a cost.

The final build figure was estimated at that point to be £1.4 million including the cost of the site. The source of funding for the land was already identified. I gave a proposal for how the balance could be raised, and from whom. This included £200,000 from Big Lottery Fund and £360,000 from trusts. Indeed, by the time we got planning permission, Big Lottery Fund was no longer supporting capital projects and in the end we raised just under £700,000 from trusts. This was an income budget written more in hope than good judgement. We had no experience of capital fundraising. But we were well known to a lot of trusts, well known locally, had run a legacy campaign several years earlier, and we could count on the support of deafblind members.

Until October 2010 we could withdraw from the offer. We would have spent approximately £73,000 which could not be recovered. Once we committed in October 2010, assuming we had detailed planning permission by that point, we could either proceed to the build stage if we had the necessary funds, or we could delay until we raised enough funds. Or, if, in the end, we were unable to raise the necessary funds, we could simply sell the land. However, a clawback clause meant we couldn't profit from selling the land for use as, say, a petrol station or a supermarket.

It seemed sensible to consider our position before finally committing to the second stage of the journey, so early in 2010 a meeting was arranged to hear 2 in-depth presentations, one making the case for completing the purchase and undertaking the building of a new centre, and-one making the case for renting a property. A business plan was presented for the new centre. After due consideration the 2007 decision to purchase the land was confirmed with the proviso that great care would be taken to ensure core funding remained intact. Later, I would more than once describe the organisational experience during this period as like riding 2 galloping horses – Russian style.

I have recounted this in a little detail taking care to maintain confidentiality as it took 3 years to get to this stage. I wanted to illustrate the very real difficulties which may need to be faced in the early stages of achieving new premises. The commitment level required from not only a board but everyone concerned, is substantial.

Chapter 18

"Field of Dreams" - The journey to planning permission

Gaining planning permission became the next target now that agreement to purchase was in place. We needed to get our new building designed, drawn up, and planning permission applied for and approved as soon as possible.

Without planning permission being in place we could not apply to large trusts and foundations for help with building a centre. So this was a priority.

In September 2010 a contract was signed and an architect was appointed. They were given the same basic remit agreed some time earlier by the Accommodation Sub-group, i.e. that a new building should be 7000–10,000 square feet, with good parking, and it should be fully accessible to deafblind people in every way, a place where they could thrive.

We then set about seeking the views of deafblind people themselves as to what they needed in the new building, in detail. A series of meetings was arranged where skilled guide/communicator support was in place to enable deafblind people to put forward suggestions on how their needs could be met, a set of very draft plans were provided and these were described to deafblind people, in the communication method of their choice.

Deafblind people wanted a building that was easy to access, where background noise was kept to a minimum, lighting was fully controllable, and good colour contrasts were used. They wanted easy external and internal journeys in and around the building which they could navigate independently.

54: Perspex building model to explore by touch

Some unusual methods were used to ensure they had a mental picture of what was envisaged, e.g. cardboard models of each room were made from old bike boxes. These were placed inside a large bike box 5ft x 2ft and moved around to show where facilities might be placed, discussions were had, and pros and cons pointed out. When requirements were clearer a scale model was made in plastic by Hammy. The fingers of deafblind individuals were guided around this plastic model on dozens of occasions. A major decision to be made was whether to build a single-storey or a 2-storey building. Eventually it was agreed that the best way to decide was to stake out the single-storey version on the actual site. Using pegs and 3-inch-wide plastic tape my son, Graeme, did this the day before Bob Nolan and his wife Louise, together with Hammy and I, arrived home from their 1000-mile Island

55: Deafblind people being guided round the site and the proposed building described to them.

Tandem trip on 16 June 2011. Then members were guided around each "room" which gave them an idea of layout and the relevant size of rooms.

Having just left George Square, Glasgow, after meeting the Provost, Bob, and Louise arrived at the site to find hundreds of red balloons being set off by a large crowd. Twenty deafblind people were then carefully guided around the outline of the proposed building and into each proposed room. A very informative happy time was had by all. This exercise was identified as a very effective way of enabling consultation with deafblind people, following the earlier use of cardboard and Perspex models.

After the site exercise it was apparent that the single-storey version of a new building felt as if it had been shoehorned into the site; it was only on the bottom end of the site that a single-storey building of any size could fit. A 2-storey building became the preferred option.

During the planning process it became apparent that there were several differing aspects to building a centre which may not always be compatible. These included the deafblind people's needs, architects' visions, neighbours' preferences, planners' regulations, funders' conditions, staff's concerns, and the New Build Group's stated limitations. All had to be taken into consideration, and a compromise reached, at different levels at different times.

In October 2011 the planning application pack was hand delivered to East Dunbartonshire Council. Three weeks later Deafblind Scotland met with the Planning Department and several items were discussed, including, the plainness of the unbroken brick wall on the Initiative Road side, the need for a high fence between the site and Larkfield Road, the desirability of moving the building eastwards and towards Initiative Road, and the coloured glass panels not being to their liking. The New Build Group had little problem in agreeing to these requests and were happy to replace the coloured glass panels with white ones. None of the changes required impinged on the accessibility of the building.

In late March 2012, planning permission was granted with several conditions imposed, 2 of which were challenging. Over the following months a good-going debate took place, until solutions were found regarding the height and type of fence to be erected between the site and Larkfield Road, and the provision of pedestrian access to the building which was a priority for the New Build Group.

Planning permission for the first design of the planned building was granted on 21 March 2013 for an 899-square-metre 2-storey building, albeit with one or 2 conditions, mainly to do with drainage, landscaping, and fencing. In the meantime, Roads Construction Consent was gained on 26 March 2013, clearing the way for full and final payment of £200,000 to be made to East Dunbartonshire Council on 28 March.

At last the "Field of Dreams" piece of land was ours. The second stage of the journey, which had lasted for 3 years, ended with that payment, and the third stage began.

Chapter 19

"Field of Dreams" - The fundraising journey

And then there was the fundraising journey. This journey had been ongoing for some time, on a smaller scale, and undertaken by individuals. We now needed to travel faster.

Essential support from deafblind people

56: Lord Provost Bob Winter welcoming Bob and Louise Nolan to George Square on the completion of LEJOG, 2008

Many people had already taken part in this momentous journey, and would continue to do so with some of the main trailblazers being deafblind people themselves. Bob Nolan and his wife Louise cycled on a tandem from Land's End to John o' Groats (the LEJOG cycle) which raised £34,500. They completed a second 1000-mile tandem ride, around 22 of Scotland's islands, raising £11,000. And then a third ride visiting each of Scotland's 7 cities, meeting lots of deafblind people, and in the process raising £3500. Bob also arranged a ceilidh in Aberdeen raising a further £4000 towards the "Field of Dreams". Bob also found the time, while working as a manager in Shell, to secure their financial support for "Field of Dreams", and also undertook his own challenges very much with their financial support. He raised more than £60,000

57: More fundraising

for "Field of Dreams". Indeed during his almost 20-year tenure as Chairperson he never stopped fundraising, undertaking a challenge most years. Louise, Abbie, and Hammy, the support team, are pictured having just received a cheque from a passer-by. Always nice!

58: John Whitfield and Leah Thom at the Grand Canyon Trek

John Whitfield, like the other deafblind fundraisers, very much enjoyed the outdoors and adventures and his first challenge was to walk the Great Wall of China – well a portion of it at least – raising £9000. He followed this with a Machu Picchu trek raising £3500, and a Grand Canyon trek raising £5000. His final challenge was the Iceland trek in 2018 raising £400. On each journey he required at least one committed guide/communicator prepared to give up their time, and to help fundraise their costs. For example, on the Great Wall of China trek he required 2 guides, Gina and Margaret, due to the number of stairs to be climbed. On the Grand Canyon trek, guide Leah accompanied John on some very difficult climbs. For deafblind people, finding a willing guide to undertake a challenge is never easy.

Stephen Joyce was an avid fundraiser for Deafblind Scotland, both for ongoing activities and "Field of Dreams". He arranged 5-a-side competitions, quiz nights etc. and ran both Edinburgh and London Marathons raising in total £7000 for "Field of Dreams". He did all of this fundraising while working full-time as Training Manager at Deafblind Scotland. We had reason to be grateful to Andrew Dewey and Don O'Brien who were his guides on the marathons. In 2014, with the help of a team from the armed services led by Captain John Vance, he climbed the 3 peaks of Ben Nevis, Scafell Pike, and Snowdon in 27 hours raising £3153.

59: Stephen Joyce and guide

Michael Anderson raised funds at a more mature age than most others, undertaking to climb Ben Nevis with guide Lucy when he was 70. Without sight and with little hearing, that was a real undertaking. He rowed 29 miles of the Forth and Clyde Canal with the help of rower David from Stirling Rowing Club. To do this he had to learn to row and then practise like mad for months. Finally, he undertook a 212-mile wild camping expedition from Iona to St Andrews – Michael's Way – with the help of Nina, which on its own raised £5000. In total he raised £10,000 for "Field of Dreams".

60: Michael Anderson

Alison Brownlie undertook a trek to Nepal, raising £3500, and then a trek to Iceland raising £5500. Alison was helped by a committed BSL interpreter, Linda McKenzie, who fundraised as well. Alison raised over £9000 for "Field of Dreams".

Agnes Fisher wrote a fascinating book, *Joy through Silence*, about her early life as a deaf person before she lost her sight, and her schooling and life experiences before and after she became deafblind. At the end of the book she says "I no longer feel limited in any way, but am strong and able to show the world that I do not think of myself as disabled. ... I no longer have that feeling of isolation that I would often experience, for through the guide/communicator service new doors have opened for me." Proceeds from sales of Agnes's book went towards "Field of Dreams". Agnes was helped in her quest to write a book by guides whose services were funded by the Numeracy and Literacy Project.

Evelyn Brown, too, benefitted from a similar project. Evelyn had little interest in English or writing at school. However, while studying childcare at college in her thirties she developed an interest in research and writing particularly about inspirational Christians she had heard about at church. To her surprise she learned some of them were blind. She also found out all about Helen Keller and learned she had visited her old school in 1932. So she wrote a 20-page large-print book titled *Inspirational People* about their contribution to society as part of Deafblind Scotland's Numeracy and Literacy project. The funds raised from sales of the book also contributed to funds for "Field of Dreams". And quotes from Evelyn's book are used in this book.

Deafblind people were important supporters of all the events we organised, taking tickets for dances and balls, and raising funds by taking part in fun runs and 10ks etc.

Essential local support

61: Field of Dreams fundraising

We had a lot of local support from East Dunbartonshire people, particularly in Kirkintilloch and Lenzie. Supporters sought sponsorship for abseils, marathons, canoeing, climbing, running 10ks, and all sorts of challenges. Local motorcyclist Steve Mason, together with friends Wilson Hutchison and Raymond Danton, travelled from South America to Alaska on the "Long Way Up" raising £7000. Individuals made donations totalling thousands of pounds. Groups did the same, e.g. Lenzie Flower Club, and Kirkintilloch Male Voice Choir who donated £2500 each from events they arranged. Rotary clubs, golf clubs, ladies groups, bridge clubs, churches, Boys Brigade companies, Girl Guides, nurseries, and schools, similarly donated funds at the end of their year.

Events

We arranged Gala balls, and dinner dances from 2012 to 2016 which raised £74,000. Businesses supported the balls taking a table, and buying auction items, while others donated items for the auction. We arranged more than one Burns Supper, several afternoon teas, at least one Ladies Lunch, and we provided a speaker for literally hundreds of groups and clubs, who subsequently donated. Thankfully hundreds of people arranged their own event or challenge in order to raise funds.

Kirkintilloch's Initiative agreed that we could have a race on the new road before it was opened to the public. Springburn Harriers, and Kirkintilloch Olympians provided the timekeeping, marshals, and lots of participants to enable this to happen. The total raised was £11,620. Carillion, who built the road, also contributed to the "Field of Dreams" fund.

We didn't start off with a mailing list of thousands as many charities do, which would have been helpful, but 75% of those already on our mailing list contributed having received our "Field of Dreams" newsletter. It was heart-warming to see how many people joined us on this mammoth journey.

62: Deafblind Scotland supporters

Garnering the support of major trusts.

However, now that we had planning permission in place we were no longer dependant only on events and sponsorship to raise funds. We could now approach trusts and foundations with a bona fide "going to happen" project they would hopefully enthusiastically support.

In the original budgeted cost of £1.4m it was expected that £360,000 could be received from trusts. We had carefully researched which Scottish trusts would potentially give to a capital project, and had come up with only a handful. However, we expanded our list, did some in-depth research, and then set about contacting them.

The trusts we had identified were initially approached in principle, then some with a proposal, and finally some with an application. Many said no, some said we will think about it, and a few said yes. In almost all cases where the approach was successful the trusts made pledges of support, with various conditions attached, the most common one being that the balance of funds needed to be in place before their particular grant could be made. Very encouragingly we were successful in interesting a number of UK trusts in funding "Field of Dreams". In the end, UK trusts were able to provide significant sums.

One interesting challenge was the differing information trusts requested. Often each trust at different times wanted different information, e.g. what funds were already in place or expected for "Field of Dreams", from what sources, what applications had been made and what rejections received, prospective funders, and what were the up-to-date project costs.

We came up with a document which quite literally listed all of this information and was regularly updated. A "Field of Dreams" paper based on this information was presented to each Finance Sub-Committee, New Build Group, and board meeting. This kept everyone informed as to the current and forecast funding situation.

Bequests and Legacies

The greatest source of funds overall was from bequests providing £960,000 in total. In 2005 directors had agreed that, going forward, any large bequests would be designated for new accommodation whenever possible and this became a significant source of funds. We had carried out a Legacy campaign using a student prior to that time which undoubtedly recruited support.

A capital project is not for the fainthearted. Raising half the funds needed will build half the building needed. It would be lovely to be able to wait until all the funding is available before starting to build. The risk is that, by that time, half the trust funding offered would no longer be available, as time limits apply. The timing needs to be carefully managed as, once given, trust funds need to be spent in a limited time, often within 1 year, so the timescale of any physical build must be adhered to in order to avoid problems.

Gordon Neasham's legacy

63 Gordon Neasham

In 2006 on a Friday afternoon, I was working with Margaret Law in a tiny rented office at number 9 Alexandra Ave when an older gentleman, smartly dressed, unassuming, came in asking about what Deafblind Scotland actually did, and for whom. Margaret and I struck up a conversation with this polite gentleman who was Gordon Neasham. Following that visit Mr Neasham came to Lenzie by train on an almost weekly basis over the next 2 to 3 months. Margaret made sure there was a scone waiting and our group of 3 enjoyed pleasant conversations about shared passions which were travelling by train, and cruising. Neither of us liked to fly and preferred to travel by train to catch the ship. He never stayed too long, maybe just half an hour, before leaving to get back on the train to Glasgow. After a few visits Mr Neasham said he had been looking for some time for a charity which might benefit from a bequest. He said he had a house and some shares as well as some money left by his brother who had died 2 years previously. Thus the relationship began which was to lead to Deafblind Scotland becoming a beneficiary in his will. Over the next year there were a few conversations to confirm arrangements and Mr Neasham phoned once or twice to ask about the shares he had donated soon after we met, and we chatted for a few minutes. And there the story ended, until the summer of 2013 when Mr Neasham died, aged 77.

I had been tempted to contact him more than once just to check how he was, but felt it might be intrusive as he may well have changed his mind, and his will. I instantly regretted that when I heard of his death. I came to regret it even more when I realised he had led a very solitary life. Little is known about Mr Neasham. He had no surviving relatives, and lived a quiet life in the west end of Glasgow. He had worked at the Western Infirmary for many years. I helped clear his flat after his death and found a wonderful store of tools, parts for model trains, and pictures of trains and cruise ships. As the flat was going on sale the following week, his solicitors Ferguson Whyte asked me to take a memento or 2 and thus a bag of his much-loved tools is in use in the O'Malley household.

In 2015, at Deafblind Scotland's 25th anniversary lunch, a cheque for £500,000 was presented by Martin Ferguson of Ferguson Whyte, with a further £99,000 arriving the following year.

Mr Neasham had been keen that, once received, the legacy should not languish in a bank account, but be quickly used for the benefit of deafblind people. The legacy arrived just when we were beginning to wonder if we would succeed in reaching our fundraising target. Indeed, we received it in 2015, which meant the actual build could hopefully start in 2016. And it did.

The contribution from sale of property

Part of the accommodation strategy in Scotland since the office opened in Barrowfield had been to purchase property, where possible, rather than rent. And when the office moved from Barrowfield, a small property in

Lenzie was bought, and others followed. This meant that in the late stages of fundraising, just before building began, the property was sold off one venue at a time, while staff were decanted in increasing numbers to a rented property in Kirkintilloch. In total £187,000 from sales of some of the property was designated to "Field of Dreams" with one property still remaining to be sold after the building was finished as it was required as a final outpost before the move.

The fundraising journey became an adventure in which we travelled hopefully, meeting success and disappointment in equal measure, and treating both as miles covered towards our destination, with the exception of for Mr Neasham's legacy, the timing of which, it has to be said, was little short of miraculous. At no point did we seriously engage with the idea of mounting a large public campaign using TV or radio or newspaper advertising. But we did investigate the cost of, and process for, all of these. Without the legacies we would have had to embark on such a campaign, or change course. Fortunately, we didn't need to.

Conclusion

In total more than £218,000 was raised from events over the period. Over £93,000 was received in donations, many of them for small amounts. Income from trusts was just under £700,000, from bequests £960,000, and from sale of property £187,000. The total raised was, in the end, £2,158,000.

Chapter 20

"Field of Dreams" - The journey to build

All the time, in parallel to the capital fundraising journey, another journey had been ongoing at a speed appropriate to the funding available. And that was the journey to a final building design, the updated planning permission needed, the accompanying building warrant to build it, and finally finding a contractor to carry out the work. Most importantly this all had to be done at a cost we could afford, and at a rate funds allowed.

In February 2015, the New Build Group met with Colin Smith to progress a project plan. Planning permission granted in 2013 would run out in 2016 so it was important to get things moving. However, costs had inevitably increased since planning permission had been granted and we were now looking at an estimated potential cost of £1,795,000 excluding land purchase costs. Colin suggested he manage a Cost Engineering Workshop to try to establish what cost savings could be made, if any.

Cutting our suit to fit the cloth

In 2015 the balance of funds for the new building was £677,000, including Mr Neasham's legacy. We had lots of promises, but not so much money in the bank. Between April and June 2015 several meetings were held to look at how, realistically, cost savings could be made. And savings were identified to potentially reduce the expected cost to around £1,481,000. But some of the suggested changes were a step too far particularly for deafblind people. The New Build Group undertook further visits to other buildings to research what cheaper options might work for us. In May, 5 people visited DBUK Peterborough to check on their experience of a new build, and how we might avoid the pitfalls. We were grateful to staff at DBUK for their honesty and support. Other sensory centres were also visited, all with a view to seeing how others had done it, possibly more cheaply.

The Design and Build process

The original design which had gained planning permission was not substantially altered in the discussions to reduce costs, so it was agreed to go out to potential contractors on a "Design and Build" basis with the original design ideas as a starting point. Design and build is a procurement method where a contractor, using his own design team, designs a building he believes can be built for a particular cost and puts in a tender to commit to this. The tenders were sent out to 7 companies in July 2015. In the meantime, we sought an extension to the existing planning permission deadline of March 2016.

In October 2015 tenders were received and interviews took place. A contractor was appointed and worked hard to find a design which would meet the needs of deafblind people at a cost we could afford. The New Build Group regularly met with them, however, we were not convinced that the design they developed would meet with the approval of Planning, Building Control, or deafblind people.

At this point the contractor was asked to stand down contractually, without penalty. However, progress had been made in that several very useful suggestions would now be incorporated in the design.

Early in 2016 the balance of funds for the new building was £980,000. The total of funds we expected to raise at that time was £1,750,000.

At that point in 2016 the New Build Group met with Colin to review the potential costs of the new building compared with the funds we knew we could raise. Costs were growing on a monthly basis. We looked at the small number of options open to us and in the end agreed to recommend the building size be reduced by 14% to 700 square metres. This would potentially bring the cost of building within immediate reach. This was a big decision as it seriously affected both the size of the activities room and the café. However, it was time to first confront reality, and second to seize the opportunity.

The end was in sight

HG Consulting put out a further set of tender documents to 4 contractors, the turnaround period to be 4 weeks. This to be done on a Design and Build basis and with the condition that building could start in August 2016 with a 12-month completion schedule.

It was considered sensible to arrange a loan facility at this juncture with a Social Investment organisation. In the end it was not necessary to use this facility, as the jigsaw of funding fell into place, but it was a very sensible precaution to take. This was not a simple process, took time to achieve, and should be considered well before it might be needed.

A major factor at this time was the issue of major pledges made by larger trusts, to all of which conditions, and a drawdown deadline, applied. Two of the main conditions to be met were that the building had to be in progress, and that the balance of funding needed had to be in place before funding could be drawn down. Only when these 2 conditions had been met could the pledged funding be requested. In addition, once the funds had been drawn down, they required to be used and accounted for within 1 year.

So we were now involved in a balancing act to try to fit together all the pieces of the jigsaw at the right time, in order to ensure all the pledges could come to fruition. One major pledge for £85,000 would expire in August 2016 so the race was on to start building in August 2016, and complete in 2017.

A contractor is appointed

In the meantime, Clark Contracts emerged as the main contractor. They met with the New Build Group on several occasions, and each time some fairly detailed discussions took place where requirements were made specific. It was felt that Clark Contracts had taken on board some of deafblind people's specific needs. And this was encouraging. They also seemed to understand the need to get the building started before the expiry date of some of the pledged funds.

On 27 June 2016, Ruth Dorman, Chief Executive, announced that a contract had been signed with Clark Contracts to build a 710-square-metre building for a fixed cost of £1,503,000, building to start in August 2016.

The project now entered the operational phase and the responsibility to oversee and deliver it was now with Project Manager Colin Smith of HG Consulting. The New Build Group, the FSC, and the Board had completed their work in getting to this stage and Colin Smith would now take forward the building as per approved plans, and decisions made. He would report to the Board, and on a day-to-day basis to Ruth Dorman, CE, and the Senior Management Team as necessary.

Throughout this time I continued to liaise with the trusts as necessary to ensure their conditions were met and each pledge was brought to fruition in a timely fashion. We were still short of funds to finish the building with all the special touches it needed e.g. light-excluding blinds for every window. And we were also £50,000 short of the build figure needed. And then a large Scottish trust who had already provided funding agreed to provide a substantial sum so that we could focus on getting the building up and running, and staff moved in, rather than worrying about how to fundraise for blinds etc. And a local housebuilding company offered to fund landscaping around the new building. Actions like this were so encouraging.

64: "Field of Dreams": first sod cut

Then came the great day. The *Kirkintilloch Herald* reported

"At the ground-breaking ceremony on 17th August vice-chair Michael Anderson cut the first sod with a ceremonial spade gifted by HG Consulting. Directors and staff were joined by provost Una Walker, councillors Rhonda Geekie, Anne Jarvis, Jim Gibbons, and Manjinder Shergill as well as local MSP Rhona Mackay, MP John Nicolson and contractor Clark Contracts of Paisley."

We all watched, fascinated, over the winter of 2016/17 as the ground was prepared, girders were delivered and erected, and the building began to take shape. In the meantime, beneath the waterline, staff were furiously paddling to make sure there would be a smooth transition from the various premises to the new building when it was finally ready for handover. Finally in June 2017 staff moved in to their new accommodation.

65: Made from Girders!

In May 2017 my husband was diagnosed with cancer and had, within days, to begin chemotherapy which continued for 6 months. It goes without saying that news like that focusses the mind very clearly on new priorities and I gave notice of my retirement as soon as we knew. Hammy had been so supportive of my work, and of Deafblind Scotland, and now the tables were turned when he needed my support which was gladly given. The chemo did the trick and he now needs only to attend annual check-ups.

A piece of good fortune

But I was able to help to arrange a very important visit before I retired, a visit which came about because of a chance meeting in 2014 when I attended the centenary celebrations of St Mary's church in Kirkintilloch. There I was introduced to the Queen's Equerry, Rear Admiral Michael Gregory. He took a great interest in Deafblind Scotland and plans for the "Field of Dreams". He suggested I get in touch when the building was about to become a reality as it might just be possible to have a member of the Royal family attend the official opening of the "Field of Dreams" – if diaries allowed.

And of course I did get in touch. And kept in touch. I filled in a form explaining why we thought a visit by a member of the Royal family would be important to deafblind people. I knew they would be thrilled to have a Royal visit. I met the representative in our local delicatessen, Billington's, as it was felt meeting in the office may raise hopes unnecessarily. It was all done very discreetly and I was advised it should be kept secret until the visit was agreed. HRH The Princess Royal could provisionally participate in a visit on one date in October. Ruth and I informed the Board of this possibility soon after, again requesting their discretion. In the interests of security, the news then remained restricted until it was broadcast by the Royal office 2 weeks before the visit which occurred on 19 October. Apparently this makes security much simpler for everyone if minimum notice is given of visits. Most of the people attending were deafblind people, and their guides, just as it should be, and Princess Anne was delighted by this.

Princess Anne was just lovely, meeting all the local dignitaries, meeting our local Singalong choir, before spending considerable time with deafblind people in the new centre. She saw every room in the building and met different deafblind people and staff in each room. She met some of the "Field of Dreams" major funders and knew some of them. But her main interest was in deafblind people, she had a long chat with several of them. And she met every guide dog. She knew about the organisation's history, its aims, what had been achieved, and what the hopes were for the future. Her grasp of detail was most impressive. She knew about the fundraising efforts of individual deafblind people and congratulated several of them. There is now a "Field of Dreams" plaque on the wall unveiled during her visit to commemorate the day.

66: HRH The Princess Royal at the "Field of Dreams" opening

From a personal point of view I was disappointed that Hammy couldn't attend due to the treatment he was receiving. But I later learned from a deafblind person and his guide that he had quietly come along and walked around the building just to see what was happening. And of course to see the motorcycles and outriders who accompanied HRH The Princess Royal's car. So he was there, and it was a deafblind person who told me, and wasn't that appropriate.

And so it was that, on 19 October 2017, Princess Anne formally opened the new Centre, to the great delight

67: HRH The Princess Royal meeting deafblind people in the activity room

of the deafblind people in attendance. A very fitting end to a very long journey which had begun more than 10 years earlier.

Including the costs of the land purchase the final cost of the new building would reach just over £2 million. "Field of Dreams" now stands like a beacon on the hill, with the Campsies in the background, if you drive along Initiative Road.

68: New building completed

Conclusion

I have written at length about the "Field of Dreams" project because being able to access the experiences of others involved in a capital project would have been really helpful in the early days. Much advice is available to charities wishing to undertake a capital project, but most of it discouraging.

This building demonstrates what deafblind people can achieve if they get the right communication support and their views are listened to. Most importantly the opening of a purpose-built centre for deafblind people in Scotland marks a significant milestone in the history of deafblindness. Hence its story belongs in this history.

SAGOD was involved at every stage in the above journey, with Michael Anderson never failing to make their voice heard or to report back to them. It is to their credit that their drive, enthusiasm, and fundraising efforts finally came to fruition in a new building. It is also to the credit of the staff and guides that they happily worked in less-than-ideal circumstances, without complaint. Life was not easy for anyone, including the Senior Management Team and the Board of Directors, for a very long period. But they prevailed. And their achievement is a purpose-built centre for deafblind people, situated in Lenzie, which has a railway station, is close to the M8, and 10 minutes from Glasgow by car.

What we did have, over a period of 10 years, was a genuine commitment from a large group of people. Outstanding among them were Bob, Michael, and Colin who never doubted that a new building could be made to happen. Each in their own way worked tirelessly to achieve it and I personally was very grateful for their indomitable spirit. The "Field of Dreams" was truly a team effort, by a team of hundreds. My advice to any charity thinking of embarking on a new capital project? Seek out such a team.

69 History boards

70: Pottery class at the new building

Chapter 21

The story of Mae Brown

71: Mae Brown and Joan MacTavish interpreting for her at university

This book began with the stories of deafblind people and their contribution to history, and it is fitting that it should end with the story of a deafblind person – Mae Brown, a young Canadian deafblind person whose life story overlapped with the era of both Helen Keller and Arthur Sculthorpe.

Mae's tutor/intervenor Joan MacTavish wrote a book titled *BRAVO! Miss Brown* which was sent to me by Joan Reynolds, guide/communicator, whose story we told earlier. Joan's note on the front said all who worked with deafblind people should read Mae's story and particularly the message from, Joan MacTavish, who wrote "No matter what your formal training or level of expertise, let the deafblind person you are assisting remain in charge and in control. At the same time, be the best stimulus, catalyst, curiosity-creator and energetic example-setter that your eyes and ears allow you to be."

Mae Brown was born on 22 May 1935 in Ontario, Canada. She was the third child in the family. Her eyesight began to deteriorate at age 2 and her hearing a few years later, and no one knew why. She walked

1.5 miles to school on a bush road on most good days. In bad weather this was impossible and her mother taught her the basics at home as best she could. Her early schooling became sporadic at best.

Her sight and hearing continued to reduce and when Mae was 13, she attended the Mayo Clinic daily. No cause was found for her sensory losses and it was thought it may be inherited. Mae's main ambition was to have a good education and, in 1950, aged 15, she began high school. However, after 6 months she had to give up; the effort was too great; her sight and hearing were so poor.

She was registered blind at age 17, and began to learn Braille. Soon afterwards Mae had a "turn" and was quickly seen by a neurologist who operated to find 2 neurofibroma, one the size of an orange, in her head. The removal of this tumour caused facial paralysis, affected her speech, her smile, and her mouth. This also removed her remaining hearing. After the operation, when Mae mouthed some questions, her mother took Mae's forefinger and wrote with it on the palm of her hand. Tactile communication thus became an integral part of Mae's future. Mae was introduced to Two-handed Manual (called Deafblind Manual in UK) and took to it like a duck to water, quickly becoming proficient.

There were no services for deafblind people in Canada at that time and appropriate support was almost impossible to find. She relied on her family, her church family, and the Canadian National Institute for the Blind (CNIB) who helped in whatever way they could. But all their expertise lay in blindness, and the loss of a single sense. When deafness is present so many possibilities for helping a blind person simply can't work.

Marjorie McGuffin-Wood was a 50-year-old deafblind person who was National Consultant on Deafblindness for CNIB. Mae was a young woman who needed and desperately wanted an education. Marjorie was committed to helping her. Within CNIB there was a growing interest in those who were deafblind. Helen Keller had been the catalyst in this new interest.

Mae's life was made tolerable by a long list of volunteers who sought to reduce her isolation, e.g. Jean Parker, who, after she heard Mae say she wished she could read a newspaper like everyone else, for 15 years brailled the week's headlines and main news and then delivered it to Mae.

In 1960 Peter Saxton, an enthusiastic, but new, volunteer reader for the blind at CNIB, was introduced to Mae. He was a busy high school teacher, impressed by Mae's enthusiasm but non-plussed by the communication problems which presented as soon as he met her. An hour later Peter was printing on her palm, and they never looked back. Peter was committed to Mae and taught her for the next 8 years, allowing her to gain the credits she needed to consider applying for a university course.

During this time Mae suffered physical problems. One evening she suffered from a really hot arm and in a short time took convulsions which resulted in hospitalisation. There were 3 or 4 tumours near her brain which had become swollen. Balancing her medication became the priority.

In an article published in 1963 Mae explained why she wanted an education, and likened her life to

> "a canyon, deep and dark, to the point of being stifling... Fresh air and the sunlight of knowledge are high above me, while I stand on the brink of defeat. To remain here would have meant certain death to the human spirit. Outside this pit was the satisfaction through academic and mental achievement. A difficult climb was the only way to the top." (Megan Easton, freelance writer, Kingston, Ontario)

In August 1964 Mae was ready to study English Literature at the grade 12 level. The more Mae studied then the more she wanted to learn. Mae was at this time also striking out in different way, she wanted a social life, conversation, to learn new skills, to dance, wine and dine, even possibly to have a relationship. John Stevenson was a shy young man. Mae wasn't shy and he and Mae became firm friends, and eventually it became a romantic relationship. They got engaged. Mae was over the moon.

John's mother lived in the UK, and as soon as she heard came over to Toronto to see them. Unfortunately, she didn't approve of the engagement and quickly arranged to take John home. He pined for Mae as soon as he reached the UK. All Mae knew was that he did not contact her again. She didn't know that his mother had told her friend "I don't want him to marry a deafblind girl." Nor did she know that his pining made him ill and inconsolable and he finally died, ostensibly from a broken heart. Mae threw herself back into her studies. Her aim was to apply to university as a mature student.

CNIB began to seek a high school teacher who could support Mae at university, someone who would be compatible with Mae. Joan MacTavish agreed to attend all lectures with Mae and Brailled material would be made available for Mae. Joan, as intervenor, would be paid $5 per hour for a maximum of 25 hours per week.

"You'll be completely on your own, Mrs MacTavish", Joan was told. "There is no precedent for this." Joan learned Deafblind Manual over the next month in preparation for meeting Mae. When Joan met Mae there was an instant rapport and Mae said "However hard you work, I'll work as hard as you do." Joan understood Mae's speech with little problem, and was quickly competent in Deafblind Manual, however, it was another step to develop speed using it.

For the next 5 years, be it attending conferences with husband Ian, or holidaying in Florida, the only books Joan read were those for Mae's courses. Joan had to learn everything the other students were learning, do it more quickly and very thoroughly in order to get it across to Mae effectively using Deafblind Manual.

Mae and Joan sat in the front row of lectures so that they could record the lecture, which Joan would replay at home, make notes from, and then ask CNIB to braille them for Mae's use. For 5 years Donnie Farley, a volunteer, transcribed these into Braille.

During the lecture Mae and Joan sat side by side Mae with her left hand across Joan's waist. Joan delivered Deafblind Manual onto Mae's left hand. It is important for both parties to find a setting which works quite well for both. There is nothing easy about using

Deafblind Manual to communicate and it can cause back problems and RSI if the comfort of both parties is not high on the agenda.

Mae's spring exam in psychology was in a multiple-choice format and her professor asked her to accept an alternative method of getting a credit. Mae refused, she wanted to do the multiple choice. Mae was told she could take as long as she liked to answer the questions. It took 15 hours over 3 consecutive days to get through the paper. By the time Joan had manualled the question and the possible answers, Mae had forgotten the question and had to have it manualled again. The exam was a real test, but not of how much she knew about the content of the psychology course.

The original idea had been that Mae would take 2 courses per year and get her degree late 1974 or early 1975. However, 8 months into her course Mae learned there were summer courses available and studying over summer could potentially enable her to achieve her degree sooner.

In January 1969 Mae and Joan sat down and mapped out how Mae might acquire the rest of her 15 credits. She then undertook some half-credit courses to speed things up. There were few books involved which avoided the perennial problem of finding volunteers who had time to do all the brailling required.

And that spring Mae had other changes on her mind. She and friend Marjorie agreed they would pool their resources and move into a flat together. This they did and Mae's enjoyment of having her own home was very apparent. She swapped recipes, cooked at weekends, and took great delight in setting her stamp on the apartment.

One of Mae's assignments as part of the Sociology course was about how deafblind people can effectively participate in society. Mae drew on her personal experiences and included what she had learned from her correspondence with Richard Kinney in Chicago, Arthur Sculthorpe in England, and Marjorie McGuffin-Wood in Canada. The world of deafblind people is incredibly small and often had a real international flavour in 1970, i.e. as long as they could read Braille.

Mae wrote at that time:

> "I do not ask for crowds of friends – just 1 or 2 here and there. All I ask is that people risk their feelings to touch me and try to talk with me. The man in the bible who lent his stable to Mary and Joseph did not so much as have his name recorded. What seemed a pretty insignificant thing to do was vitally important as things turned out."

In January 1972 Mae heard that from 1 September 1972 she would be employed as a counsellor for the deafblind in Ontario division. Mae's dream of being employed would come true. She was overjoyed.

It had taken Mae 60 months to achieve the necessary credits, instead of the normal 24. And it had taken 12 years in total to reach her graduation in Convocation Hall, 7 years of preparation, and 5 years at university.

Mae graduated on 1 June 1972. The graduation was televised by CBC. Mae and Joan had agreed that whatever happened they would keep their heads and do what was expected of us. They had rehearsed the walk, the stairs, the number of steps to the Chancellor so they would look little different from anyone else. Mae sat at the front to avoid all the steps from the student section. Mae was the last to be called. As if they had done it every day of their lives, they walked steadily up the 3 steps and took 5 paces forward to kneel before the Chancellor. In near total silence Chancellor McGibbon printed clearly on Mae's outstretched palm "Admitto Te" and she stood up to thunderous applause, none of which she could hear.

There then followed a round of parties and celebrations which Mae thoroughly enjoyed. She was introduced wherever she went as the "first deafblind person in Canada to graduate" and the first woman since Helen Keller who in 1904 had received her degree at the age of 24. Twenty-four was Mae's age when she first began her education by getting high school lessons from Peter Saxton. Mae's graduation was in newspapers in cities across Canada and America and indeed across the world.

Mae began her new role with CNIB on 1 September 1972. As a deafblind professional in a hearing world it was far from easy. Joan worked as part-time secretary 3 mornings per week for a year and then moved on. Mae had a notice which said "Touch me, it is the only way I will know you have come to see me." Joan was a first-class intervenor, few others at that time could fill this role. But Mae was determined to fulfil her ambition of a specialist service for deafblind people. Her working life could be very lonely. Communication with others was never going to be easy or relaxed.

Sharing a flat with Marj, who could use Deafblind Manual, was helpful.

She started a newsletter for deafblind people called *The Communicator*. In CNIB's terms deafblind people were those with a severe sight and hearing loss who could not use verbal communication and this was the group Mae was working with. Mae set out to help adults who used Two-handed Manual get together to communicate, which was not easy in a country the size of Canada, but they succeeded in doing so 2 or 3 times a year, and local groups continued to meet almost monthly.

Early in 1973 Mae was beginning to see the fruits of her labours, as most agencies she had been in contact with were now beginning to provide services for adults as well as for children. The specialist service she wanted was no longer a dream. She was in touch with others doing similar work, producing a newsletter to inform, training CNIB people, and researching and testing devices to suit deafblind people. Despite the difficulties progress was being made on a number of fronts.

Mae had also become keen to try living alone, just to be fully independent and Marj and Mae finally agreed that Marj would move out in February 1973.

Mae's physical health was suffering and her doctor advised she focus on the positives the way she always had and get on with her life. She threw herself into work with a new drive. In the meantime, Mae was quietly visiting the nurse, Earline, more frequently due to dizziness and headaches. She said to Earline that she thought her time was short but she was not afraid, her faith led her to believe she would begin a new life where she could see and hear again. Earline suggested she express her thoughts in a poem, and she did, several of them, one of which, "A Raindrop in Distress", is reprinted below.

On Sunday 4 November Joan received a phone call from Marjorie, which was not uncommon, but Joan knew right away from Marj's voice that all was not well. However, she was totally unprepared for the news Marjorie broke to her. Mae had died suddenly a short time before. Marjorie said Mae had just dropped to the floor as she was walking down the hall to her bedroom. Joan cried down the phone "No, no, she cant be." She was overwhelmed by the unfairness of it all. Mae had accomplished so much, but still had so much to do. She was just 38 years old.

Just as newspapers across Canada, America, and the world had reported Mae's graduation, they reported her death in a similar vein: "First deafblind graduate from a Canadian university dies." On 16 November Joan wrote to Arthur Sculthorpe in England to tell him about Mae's death. Arthur himself died a few months later, but not before Joan had managed to see him while in England on a working trip with her husband.

Mae wrote many poems; this one was written just months before her death.

> "A Raindrop in Distress
> A frantic little raindrop
> Deserted by a shower
> All shimmering a tremble
> Like a bashful summer flower
> Clung just above the rooftop

To a faithful oaken limb
While autumn leaves fell to his feet
As if they worshipped him
The gathered clouds had met and gone
After a moment's fun
But the frightened little raindrop
Still glistened in the sun
The leaves looked on astonished
At the raindrop's fearful plight
And watched her faithful oaken friend
As day became the night
At last the weary raindrop knew
She too her friend must leave
And slipped into the barrel
Placed below the wooden eave
Among the millions of other raindrops
Awaiting it to fall
Our courageous little raindrop
Was not alone at all."

Joan MacTavish went on to become Co-ordinator Deafblind Services for CNIB thus continuing the work Mae had begun. By 1981 it is recorded that Ontario's 70 intervenors could provide 3 hours per week of Intervenor services to 180 deafblind adults. Later, intervenors in Toronto developed their own organisation, code of ethics, standards etc.

On a day when someone suggests it's unrealistic for a deafblind person to expect to get a job, a partner, a degree, start a specialist service for deafblind people – remember the story of Mae Brown, and ask them to think again.

(Information for this chapter is from *BRAVO! Miss Brown: A world without sight and sound 1935–1973* by Joan MacTavish, published by Cavu Inc., Canada, distributed by Hushion House Publishing Inc., 2001.)

Bibliography

Axelrod, C., *And the Journey Begins,* Douglas McLean, Coleford, Gloucestershire.
Quotations used from pages 18, 187, 189, 190, 196, 199, 200

Brown, E., *Inspirational People,* Deafblind Scotland, 2010
Quotations used from page 16

Carroll, C. and Fischer, C.H., *Orchid of the Bayou: a deaf woman faces blindness,* Gallaudet University Press, Washington, DC, 2001
Quotations used from pages 26, 232

Chambers, D., *Words in my hands,* Ellexa Press LLC, Colorado, 2012
Quotations used from pages 201, 233

Fisher, A., *Joy Through Silence,* Gordon Fisher, Ayr, 2012
Quotation from page 67

Freeberg, E., *The education of Laura Bridgemen,* The President and Fellows of Harvard College, 2002
Quotation used from page 34

MacTavish, J., *Bravo! Miss Brown: A world without sight and sound 1935 – 1973,* Cavu Inc, Canada, 2001
Quotations used from Foreword, pages132, 150, 160, 161,240, 287, 299, 372, 273, 379, 332.

Reid, T., Thomas Reid's *Inquiry and Essays* (ed. R.E. Beanblossom and K Lehrer) Hackett Publishing, Indianapolis, 1983
Quotations used from pages 31–35

Wardrop, J., *History of James Mitchell: A boy born blind and deaf, with an account of the operation performed for the recovery of his sight,* John Murray, London, 1813; reprinted Kessinger Publishing 2010
Quotation used from page 12

List of Photographs

17. Bob and Louise Nolan, 2012 Olympic torch relay in Banchory.
18. John Whitfield in DbS office.
19. Irene Birse taken at SAGOD first meeting, Tom Johnson House, Kirkintilloch, October 1997.
20. Michael Anderson.
21. Maria Crawford.

Chapter 3

22. Frank Thomson.
23. Desmond Smith at DBUK Peterborough event in the 90s.
24. Francis Keane with John Dearie at a "Doers" Christmas meal 1997.
25. John Dearie at a chess competition in Germany 2004.
26. Clark Steven in Celtic Park.
27. Clark Steven and C. Lawler being recorded for Celtic TV
28. John Smith
29. 2005 March, Anne Dobbie. Margaret Mitchell MSP, M. Tervitt, Michael Anderson and David McLetchie MSP.
30. 2005 March Drena O'Malley and Mike Hooper with banners, followed by others, George IV Bridge, Edinburgh.

Chapter 4

31. Drena O'Malley and Clark Steven in Alexandra Avenue Lenzie. Pictures courtesy of Sunday Mail Newspaper and photographer Victoria Stewart
32. Chapter 8 NDBL's Aberdeen group pictured in early 50s on a trip to Huntly. Courtesy of Anne Barnett retired CE of DBUK, now deceased

33. The Scottish team when we moved to Lenzie in 1994. Wendy Forrest, Anne Barnett, Drena O'Malley, John Frame, Ellen Cattanach.
34. Anne Barnett with Dorrie Moore at the opening of 21 Alexandra Avenue.

Chapter 9

35. Sanja Tarczay, CE of Croatia Association of Deafblind, at the Forum in 2004 in Golden Lion, Stirling. Showing Andrew Dewey BSL interpreter, Croatian Interpreter, Michael Anderson, Sanja Tarczay

Chapter 10

36. Deafblind Studies Diploma Group at 2004 graduation with Bob Peckford, Mark Gray, Michael Anderson, Ken Halsworth, Virginia Von Malachowsky, Jackie Smith, Gill Morbey, Sarah Breslin, Margaret Law, Drena O'Malley and Sense Scotland students.
37. Gill Morbey and Drena O'Malley lobbying for "Yes to Access" campaign, 1999/2000 at the Assembly Rooms, Edinburgh.

Chapter 11

38. Jill McDonald, staff member, looking at the G/C board in Lenzie office, and considering her options.

Chapter 12

39. Joan Reynolds
40. Margaret-Anne Duthie at a SAGOD meeting interpreting for W. Taylor
41. 10th anniversary celebration in City chambers, showing, Drena O'Malley, Bob Nolan, Jackie Hicks (CE of DBUK)

Chapter 13

42. Hands around Scotland group at Aberdeen airport with Irene Birse, Bob Nolan, George Simpson, John Whitfield, and Kate Fraser.
43. Hands around Scotland group at SECC 2001. Seen in the picture are Stephen Joyce, J. Dearie, D. O'Malley and an open top bus full of deafblind people, and a piper.

Chapter 14

44. March 2005 group at Waverley Station, Edinburgh. Rogan Welsh, Allan Clark and several placards are identifiable.
45. March 2005 Margaret Mitchell MSP, Bob Nolan, D. O'Malley outside Scottish Parliament
46. March 2005 Irene Birse outside parliament with Andrew Welsh, her MSP
47. Picture taken in the Scottish Parliament cafe with Scott G/C, Stephen Joyce, Robert Dillon, Ken Halsworth G/C, Willie Dixon G/C, Drena O'Malley and Desmond Smith.

Chapter 15

48. Mark Griffin MSP with Stephen Joyce celebrating the vote on the BSL Bill
49. Drena O'Malley with Hilary Third from the Equality Unit celebrating the inclusion of tactile communication

Chapter 17

50. Office Premises at 21,25,27 Alexandra Avenue.
51. Picture of two tenement flats, one up, which DbS owned at 23 Alexandra Avenue.
52. Aerial photograph of the "Field of Dreams" site courtesy of Kirkintilloch's Initiative Archive

53. Picture of a muddy field taken by Drena on her first site visit.

Chapter 18

54. A Perspex building model made by Hammy which enabled deafblind people to explore by touch where rooms might be
55. Picture of the FOD site pegged out as the proposed building with deafblind people being guided round having the building described to them.

Chapter 19

56. Lord Provost Bob Winter with Bob and Louise Nolan in George Square after LEJOG June 15th 2008.

Chapter 20

57. Louise and Abbie give Hammy a donation from a passer-by through the van window on LEJOG.
58. John Whitfield and Leah Thom on the Grand Canyon Trek using a chain rope to navigate a difficult climb.
59. Stephen ran the Edinburgh Marathon more than once, on this occasion with Andrew Dewey as his guide/communicator.
60. Michael Anderson rowing 39 miles along the Forth and Clyde Canal.
61. "Field of Dreams" 10k and 5k Runs. Courtesy of Carillion
62. "The Three Amigos" are pictured during their fundraising ride from South America to Alaska.
63. Gordon Neasham, benefactor Courtesy of Ferguson Whyte
64. Ground breaking ceremony performed by Michael Anderson assisted by R. Dorman and D. O'Malley

65. Made from Girders! The girders were delivered and erected within days – or so it seemed.
66. HRH The Princess Royal officially opening the new "Field of Dreams" Centre 20th October 2017 with Ruth Dorman and deafblind people and guides
67. HRH The Princess Royal meeting deafblind people in the activity room. Speaking to John Dearie through a Deafblind Manual Interpreter. Both photographs by Jeff Holmes, courtesy of 3x1 Consultancy
68. The new Learning and Development Centre completed
69. Thanks to Heritage Lottery Funding a Very Large Print History has been created in the new corridor
70. Alison Dunbar and Helen McGoldrick practicing their pottery skills in the new Learning and Development Centre.

Chapter 21

71. Mae Brown and Joan MacTavish interpreting for her at university. From Bravo Miss Brown book. Cava inc Canada

I am grateful to all who have taken photographs and given me permission to use them

Printed in Great Britain
by Amazon

37144727R00163